Women in a world perspective

Women as heads of households in the Caribbean: family structure and feminine status

Joycelin Massiah
Deputy Director,
Institute of Social and Economic Research,
University of the West Indies,
Bridgetown, Barbados

Unesco

The author is responsible for the choice and the presentation of the facts contained in this book and for the opinions therein, which are not necessarily those of Unesco and do not commit the Organization.

Published in 1983 by the United Nations Educational,
Scientific and Cultural Organization,
7 place de Fontenoy, 75700 Paris
Printed by Spottiswoode Ballantyne Ltd,
Colchester, Essex

ISBN 92-3-102047-1

Printed in the United Kingdom

Preface

This monograph presents the findings of a country case-study carried out within the Population Division's programme on 'Studies on the Status of Women in relation to Development and Demographic Behaviour'. Research on the status of women has broadened its perspectives to include an exploration of the differential effects of social and economic development upon the condition of women. The principal aim of this research programme is to identify relationships between socio-economic development and demographic trends and to analyse their impact on women's role within the family, their participation in the labour force, and migration and fertility patterns. There are evidently enormous national as well as regional differences in women's position in the family and their social and economic status, and these studies are designed to elucidate the precise nature of those differences and their implications for women and development in the countries concerned.

This particular study, carried out by Joycelin Massiah, throws new light upon the relatively high incidence of female-headed households in the Caribbean, where they constitute no less than one-third of the total number of households in the region. It offers some valuable insights into the composition of such households, the reasons for their existence, their problems and the multiple survival strategies employed by women in such a position. The findings show that female heads of households are concentrated in low-paid, low-status occupations with no prospects. The study confirms that women who head households are more disadvantaged than men in a similar position. However, measures adopted with a view to ameliorating the situation would need to increase the economic opportunities available to both men and women, since severe constraints upon their earnings possibilities affect men and women alike in their capacity to contribute to a household.

This study will be of value to development planners, since it clearly indicates that policy-makers have a choice between rehabilitation or sustenance; sustenance imposes a heavy burden on the region's meagre welfare resources and perhaps perpetuates an unsatisfactory situation, while rehabilitation involves the development of programmes directed specifically towards women, which should include the provision of child-care facilities, training in non-traditional areas of occupation, and expanding opportunities for part-time work, as well as devising income-generating programmes which would enable women to work from within the household. This might allow women who head households to manage without recourse to public welfare and might even diminish the rising incidence of this phenomenon.

Contents

1 Introduction

Historical background

Recent evidence from census and survey data dealing with the position of women in different societies has pointed to the growing incidence of female-headed households, particularly in developing countries [37].[1] This increase appears to be closely correlated with processes of modernization arising from specific forms of economic-development strategies. One recent report provides striking evidence of the negative effect of such strategies on women in general, and on those who head households in particular [8]. That report, which is based on aggregate census data, contains a significant section on the Commonwealth Caribbean using material from the 1970 population census supplemented by an overview of some of the anthropological literature on the Caribbean family. According to the report, the Caribbean data provide 'compelling evidence of the disadvantaged position of women who are heads of households as compared both to the female population in general, and to the population of men who are household heads in particular' [8, p. ii].

Without attempting to initiate a lengthy discussion on the origins of this phenomenon, it is important to note that this has been a feature of West Indian family life from the earliest days of its history. Under the slave regime the basic elements necessary to the sharing and maintenance of a common household by a legally married couple were unavailable to the slaves. Christian marriage was incompatible with the slave code: each partner was at the risk of being removed or sold at any time. The child of a slave woman derived status from its mother's legal status, thus automatically becoming the property of its mother's owner. Efforts

1. The figures in brackets refer to the entries in the list of references at the end of the book.

at stimulating reproduction often took the form of special dispensations to the mother and to the plantation overseers or managers but never to the fathers. Such practices had the effect of giving legitimacy to the centrality of the mother's role, a notion that was firmly entrenched in the kin systems of the West African tribes transported to the New World.

Recent data suggest that such practices did not necessarily serve to introduce and perpetuate the notion of male marginality. Using data for Jamaica, Trinidad and Tobago, and Barbados, Higman has demonstrated that young slave women tended to live either in a childless co-residential union or in an extended family household group. During the prime reproductive years, the majority of slave women lived with a mate and their children. After their children set up independent households, the woman reverted to living only with her mate or, if he died, with her children in some version of the extended family [22]. Available evidence of slave mortality patterns suggests that with an expectation of life of only twenty-three years towards the end of slavery [41], large numbers of women surviving to establish 'grandmother' households could hardly be expected. Higman's data indicate that household units consisting of a woman and her children ranged from 14 per cent in Jamaica to 29 per cent in Trinidad and Tobago, suggesting that the incidence of women-headed households was firmly established during slavery but was perhaps not as extensive as common opinion would have us believe.[1]

The second set of factors that may be said to have contributed to the existence of female-headed households in the region is related to migration. In other societies migration has also been cited as an important contributory factor, but the emphasis is on internal migration. In the Caribbean, although rural-urban migration is undoubtedly important, the more crucial type of migration from the perspective of this study is external migration. This has been a feature of Caribbean societies from the earliest days, assuming particular prominence from about the third quarter of the nineteenth century. Indeed, except for the short period from the late 1920s to the early 1940s, the past hundred years or so have witnessed a steady exodus from the region, the direction and volume of the movement changing as people's perceptions of available opportunities changed. It may now be said that an emigration ethic has become an integral aspect of the culture, in the sense that emigration is now accepted as a valid life option. Until recently this has been an essentially male phenomenon that has had significant implications for the female population. Successive migration streams attracted ever larger numbers of males,

1. Conversely, between 36 per cent and 54 per cent of units were simple family households or childless co-residential units, implying that households characterized by the absence of a male were not necessarily the norm.

thereby producing marked imbalances between the sexes within the productive and reproductive ages. In Barbados, for example, the sex ratio for this group moved from 715 in 1891 to 526 in 1921, i.e. during a period marked by heavy sex-selective emigration. Between 1921 and 1946, the male deficit in the population was considerably reduced, the sex ratio rising to 845 during this period of minimal migration. A resurgence of emigration during the decade of the 1950s produced declines in the sex ratio, which by 1960 stood at 809. After 1960 the trend was once again reversed, and a rise to 903 in the sex ratio of this age-group resulted. This feature is particularly interesting, since emigration during this period involved considerable numbers of females, thus contributing to a decline in the traditional balance of the sex ratio in favour of the females. The continued deficit of males in this crucial age-range meant that significant numbers of females were required to manage their households single-handedly. It may be argued that it was during this period that the phenomenon of female household heads took firm root in the region.

Another series of reasons given for the incidence of female-headed households in the region centres on notions of increased female independence as socio-economic conditions improve. One manifestation of this independence is to be found in the adoption of the non-residential sexual union as a socially acceptable option rather than a deviant alternative. One recent study[1] in which the characteristics of women in visiting unions were explored concludes:

> A careful consideration of views of respondents points definitely to their position that this form of family accords them a degree of freedom and independence which they hold to be greatly to their advantage. Even from the standpoint of the support of their children and the family as a whole, they maintain that the absence of the partner is by no means a disaster. For economically they do not consider their position unduly difficult; such financial assistance as they receive from their partners has not to be spent in partial support of the latter, as would be the case in residential unions. Such funds serve solely for their own support and for the upkeep of their children. [43, p. 249]

In effect the respondents in the Jamaica study stress clear advantages to being in the visiting union, and by extension to managing their own households. These include the assurance of freedom and a measure of independence, qualities that appear to be highly valued.

1. In contrast to the census definition, this study characterizes a visiting union by the existence of a steady sexual relationship between partners, the maintenance of separate households and the lack of legal sanction of the union. Most such women lived in households consisting of themselves and their children: i.e. they were female heads of household [43].

Reference to the high incidence of female household headship in the region has been made in the extensive literature on lower-income black families in the Caribbean, much of which concerns itself with the notion of matrifocality.[1] It is not proposed to enter the controversy about what constitutes matrifocality, which is here used to describe a concept denoting that the role of the mother is structurally, culturally and effectively centred [52]. 'Female-headed households' is here used to describe a wide range of domestic arrangements typified mainly by the absence of an adult male in the relation of spouse or partner of the dominant female and in which the basic structural principle is the conjugal link between members. Such households may be two- or three-generational units, being analogous to what Laslett defines as 'simple family households' or 'extended family households' respectively [27, pp. 29–30]. The important distinguishing feature is not only that the dominant female assumes responsibility for the affairs of a household consisting of herself, her children and/or her grandchildren, but also that her position as head of the household is recognized and admitted as such by all household members. Some writers use demographic arguments to account for the reportedly high incidence of such households in the Caribbean—the greater the surplus of females, the higher the proportion of female household heads [39]; others use economic arguments—where a high proportion of males are unable to obtain jobs at wage levels that permit the maintenance of household groups, females appear as household heads [19]. One of the earliest works on West Indian family structure, however, stresses the importance of viewing this phenomenon within the context of the woman's life cycle [47]. Smith attributes the incidence to economic insecurity and the marginality of low-income groups to the general economic system.

Despite the fact that the literature suggests that female household headship has been a characteristic feature of lower-income family life, no attention seems to have been given to the study of this particular form of household arrangement from the perspective of the woman. The present work is concerned, not with the determinants of female-headed households, but with an elaboration of the characteristics of females who head households, the problems they face and the strategies they develop to cope with their circumstances. Three sources of data are used: the 1970 Population Census serves to develop a demographic profile of women in the Caribbean who head households; data from a small pilot study concerned with the Role of Women in the Caribbean are used to demonstrate the kinds of problems and the survival strategies

1. For studies in which specific reference is made to female household headship as distinct from the issue of matrifocality, see especially 13, 23, 39, 47, 57. For a detailed listing of studies on the West Indian family see 30.

adopted by these women in three territories—Barbados, Jamaica, and Trinidad and Tobago;[1] and data from National Assistance records from one territory, Barbados, are used to demonstrate one type of governmental response to the plight of the poorest of these women. Policy implications are discussed in the final section.

A question of definition

It is useful to examine the various forms female-headed households may take. In Western societies women who head households are usually categorized in terms of their marital status and are therefore identified as being either widowed, divorced or separated. Widowhood is not regarded as being an important contributor to female households. The crucial factor is often cited as marital instability. According to Sawhill, in the United States of America increasing economic opportunities for women outside of marriage and changing attitudes towards women's roles in society have resulted in women opting either out of an unsatisfactory marriage or not marrying at all [45]. Indications that this trend may be imminent in the Caribbean are evident for Barbados, where between 1948 and 1975 the annual number of divorce petitions and the number of decrees granted more than tripled, while the annual number of marriages increased by only one-fifth. Simultaneously the divorce rate increased from 1.4 per 100 marriages in 1948 to 6.2 in 1960 and 12.9 by 1975. An interesting sidelight on these figures is that up to the 1960s the number of divorce petitions presented by husbands exceeded that presented by wives. However, by the 1970s this position was completely reversed, so that by 1975 wives presented more than twice the number of petitions presented by husbands [17]. Without similar evidence from other parts of the region a case for increases in marital instability cannot be clearly made. Indeed, census data indicate that among female household heads a mere 2 per cent may be categorized as divorced or legally separated.[2]

A much more important category in the Caribbean is the widowed group, which accounted for proportions ranging from 34.1 per cent

1. This pilot study took the form of a pre-test in which a questionnaire designed to elicit information centring around the themes emotional support, sources of livelihood, power and authority, was administered to a test group of twenty-eight respondents. The focus of the study was not on female household headship but on the role of women generally. Relevant data from the ten women who claim to be household heads are utilized in this book.
2. The range is from 6.0 per cent in the Turks and Caicos Islands to 0.5 per cent in St Lucia.

(Guyana) to 11.4 per cent (St Vincent) of females who head households in the region. In societies in which life expectancy is continually increasing and continually in favour of females and where the difference between the mean age of spouses at marriage is no greater than five years, a tendency towards high numbers of widowed females would be expected. In Jamaica, for example, male life expectancy increased from 35.9 years in 1921 to 62.2 years in 1960, while female life expectancy moved from 38.2 to 66.3 over the same period. In 1960 the average age at marriage for Jamaican females aged 15–49 was 30.9 years and that for males aged 15–59 was 35.2 years. If a woman aged 15 years married a man five years her senior the probability that he would survive until she attained age 50 was 0.88, whereas the probability that she would survive until he attained age 50 was 0.93. In short, women are more likely than men to outlive their spouses. Further, as in many societies, despite the absence of specific cultural taboos against widows re-marrying or of specific institutional support for widows, there is nevertheless a marked tendency towards a low remarriage rate of widowed women. Such women are therefore forced to maintain separate households for themselves and their children.

In the Caribbean the majority of women who head households have never been married, but have been in a male/female union of some kind previously. In some female-headed households there may be a resident male in the husband/partner relationship, but he is unable to function as the household head for health or economic reasons. In such cases the male's inability to sustain his economic role effectively results in the deterioration of his status within the household, and a female-headed household develops with the woman retaining control over such income and assets as she may have and over her children.

Whether a male partner is absent or not, it is important to recognize that female-headed households need not include children, although those involving children predominate. The point is important in a region in which mortality levels and patterns are closely approaching those prevailing in the developed world. Women are therefore enjoying a greater longevity, and a considerable number of older women are electing to live alone as 'solitaires', to use Laslett's terminology—a feature that contains specific implications for social welfare.

The question of what constitutes a female-headed household is integrally linked with the particular definitions adopted for the concepts 'household' and 'head of household'. Following recommended United Nations procedures, the three most recent censuses of the Commonwealth Caribbean devised the following definitions:

A Private Household is defined as one or more persons voluntarily living together and sharing at least one daily meal. In general, a household comprises a father, mother, children, other relatives, as well as other persons sharing in their household arrangements. . . . It is important to note, however, that a member of the household is not necessarily a member of the family, nor will all members of the family be members of the household. It is also important to note that a household may include more than one family [53].

A clear distinction is therefore made between 'household', which is construed in terms of domestic arrangements, and 'family', which is defined in terms of kin relationships. It is an important distinction and one that tends to be obscured in the current literature on female-headed households.

Another definition worthy of repetition is that relating to the term 'head of household', which for the recent regional censuses[1] has been:

The head of the household is generally the person who is responsible for the upkeep and maintenance of the household—usually the husband or common-law husband. Where the husband or common-law husband is not the head, or where no man lives in the household, *the person who claims the position* [emphasis added] or who is so regarded by other members of the household is treated as head [53].

This approach served three basic purposes in the recent censuses in the region. Initially, it provided the census enumerator with a focal point for the collection of information from the household, in that the head of the household could invariably provide most of the required information for all household members. Secondly, the characteristics of the household are linked to the person designated as head. This facilitates cross tabulations of household features with demographic and social characteristics of the person who is head. Thirdly, the last two censuses used the head-of-household schedule for the collection of information on household amenities and characteristics of the dwelling unit. While these data were not tabulated according to head of household, the procedure permitted the conduct of a simultaneous population and housing census—a considerable economic saving.

Despite these obvious advantages it is evident that by leaving the matter to be settled by the respondent, rather than instructing the enumerator to categorize on the basis of a specific criterion—presumably responsibility for upkeep and maintenance of the household—a distinct cultural bias is introduced into the data. In the Caribbean, where matrifocality of the family is stressed but male authoritarianism is the ideal, there may well be a tendency to overstate male headship. By contrast, where the allocation relies on the 'person who claims the position', it becomes possible for a woman to cite herself, in

1. These definitions were retained for the 1970 and 1980 censuses.

the absence of her husband/partner at the time of enumeration. Whether either of these biases is sufficient to offset the other is impossible to tell. However, in a region in which women have traditionally assumed important roles, data on household heads by sex are regarded as an important input into national social planning. Thus, in contrast to other regions, such as the countries of the Economic Commission for Europe, which have opted to discontinue the compilation of tabulations based on the characteristics of the household head, the thrust in the Caribbean is for a more reliable and wider range of such tabulations.

Whatever our dissatisfactions with the available census definitions, it must be remembered that an enumeration exercise dealing with thousands or millions of persons cannot realistically be expected to include as many refinements of conceptualization as we would wish. Further, little methodological research has been conducted with a view to devising viable alternatives to the 'head of household' concept. Where it has, the experience has been that results differ little from previous censuses that adopted the head-of-household approach. This has been the experience, for example, of the 1980 United States Population and Housing Census, which adopted the notion of 'reference person', defined as the 'person in whose name the home is owned or rented' [54]. In effect, all the census data can offer are gross indicators of headship, however defined. More precise indicators must rely on micro-level data. At that level, it becomes possible to treat such issues as the diversity of household structures, the determinants of different types, the nature and allocation of authority within different types and the linkage between differential household types and the politico-economic structures in which they are embedded.

2 Demographic profile of female-headed households in the Caribbean

Data from the 1970 census permit, for the first time, a detailed comparative analysis of the characteristics of household heads. Published summary tables on the non-institutional population adopt sex of head as a control variable, separately cross-tabulated by age, educational attainment, marital status, main activity, occupational group and annual income. One tabulation shows female household heads by union status. Some of the tabulations are three-way tables, showing the relevant variable, size of household and number of rooms. Others are two-way tables showing the relevant variable and type of dwelling. All tabulations are presented separately by sex of head. Virtually all of the tabulations are presented at national level, but a few disaggregate at the major division level (i.e. well-defined geographical/administrative units) and others at the major and minor division (i.e. subdivisions within each major division) level, but none appear at the Enumeration District (ED) level. The only marginally comparable material from an earlier census was in 1960, when an ED table on number of families by size and sex of head of family was published. The task of reconstructing family units proved too formidable to be repeated in 1970 and 1980; hence the focus on head-of-household data. At least two studies have made use of some of the 1970 household data.[1] Here we attempt to take both of those studies a step further.

For the region as a whole, Table 1 shows that about 32 per cent of household heads are female, with the highest proportions recorded for St Kitts (46.6 per cent) and lowest for Guyana (22.4 per cent). Of the fourteen territories, eight record proportions higher than 40 per cent,

1. Figures in the two studies vary somewhat, since the Buvinić study [8] excludes single-person households. Because a large proportion of such households relate to women aged 65+, who therefore represent a specific welfare problem, the Massiah study [28] includes them.

TABLE 1. Various characteristics of household heads

Territory	Proportion of households headed by women	Median age of female household heads	Mean size of households headed by women	Proportion of female household heads never married	Proportion of female household heads not in union	Proportion of female household heads with only primary education	Proportion of female household heads in work force	Index of dissimilarity of occupations
	%			%	%	%	%	
Jamaica	33.8	48.9	3.9	62.4	47.9	92.4	40.0	48.4
Trinidad and Tobago	27.0	51.0	4.1	34.9	48.1	89.2	30.6	39.0
Guyana	22.4	49.7	4.5	29.8	55.9	90.7	31.1	47.3
Barbados	42.9	54.9	3.7	54.3	41.9	47.5	45.5	43.2
Belize	24.8	48.4	4.7	44.1	43.2	93.8	28.4	54.1
St Lucia	40.9	48.7	4.1	56.3	38.7	96.6	39.8	31.3
Grenada	45.3	52.4	4.5	58.3	46.8	95.5	45.4	22.0
St Vincent	45.4	49.3	4.9	67.3	36.1	96.8	38.7	24.9
Dominica	42.4	50.3	4.1	57.1	48.2	96.0	44.1	30.7
St Kitts/Nevis	46.6	51.4	4.1	59.7	44.3	93.8	40.8	33.5
Montserrat	43.7	58.6	3.4	59.9	44.8	96.1	34.5	40.7
British Virgin Islands	24.3	46.3	4.0	47.4	41.4	88.6	44.2	66.3
Cayman Islands	35.5	52.2	4.7	32.2	30.4	89.9	34.8	62.3
Turks and Caicos	40.3	44.6	4.0	32.1	33.9	93.2	35.2	33.8
Mean	32.0		4.0		47.5	88.3	37.9	41.8
High	46.6	54.9	4.9	67.3	55.9	96.8	45.5	66.3
Low	22.4	44.6	3.4	29.8	30.4	47.5	30.6	22.0

Source: Tables 1 to 10 are derived from: University of the West Indies, Census Research Programme, *1970 Population Census of the Commonwealth Caribbean*, Vol. 9, 'Housing and Households', Kingston, 1975.

TABLE 2. Proportional distribution of female household heads by marital status, 1970

Territory	Never married	Married	Widowed	Divorced or separated	Total
	%	%	%	%	
Jamaica	62.4	18.9	16.5	2.2	142 000
Trinidad and Tobago	34.9	32.3	29.7	3.1	52 000
Guyana	29.8	30.4	34.1	5.8	28 900
Barbados	54.3	24.3	19.4	2.0	25 100
Belize	44.1	33.7	20.7	1.5	5 700
St Lucia	56.3	24.1	19.3	0.5	8 900
Grenada	58.3	19.3	20.0	2.5	8 900
St Vincent	67.3	20.3	11.4	1.0	7 700
Dominica	57.1	21.4	19.6	1.8	6 400
St Kitts/Nevis	59.7	22.7	16.1	1.5	5 200
Montserrat	59.9	20.5	17.6	2.0	1 400
British Virgin Islands	47.4	28.1	20.7	3.9	600
Cayman Islands	32.2	36.4	25.5	5.9	900
Turks and Caicos	32.1	33.3	28.6	6.0	500
					294 200
High	67.3	36.4	34.1	6.0	
Low	29.8	18.9	11.4	0.5	

and three record proportions of 25 per cent and less. In general, countries with a significantly large black population are those recording a high proportion of female-headed households, while the converse holds for countries with significant proportions of East Indians (Trinidad, Guyana) or native Indians (Belize). One territory, British Virgin Islands, which is known to have a very high proportion of migration affecting both sexes, also reflects relatively low proportions.

The median age for both sexes is well over 40 years for all territories, with females reflecting consistently higher median ages than males in all but two cases. Indeed in two territories—Guyana and the Caymans—the median age for females is about eight years higher than that for males. Much of this can probably be explained in terms of the prevailing pattern of mortality, in which females survive males at the higher end of the age range. In fact, well over one-third of female single-person households consist of women over 65 years of age, and in the Turks the proportion rises to as high as 54 per cent.

Male and female household heads in the Caribbean maintain households of approximately similar size. In general, male-headed households tend to be somewhat larger than female ones, the average for the fourteen territories being 4.8 for males and 4.0 for females. Largest household sizes are recorded at 5.7 for males in Guyana and 4.9 for females in St Vincent. Lowest for both sexes are evident in Montserrat, where the value for males is 3.5 and for females 3.4.

TABLE 3. Proportional distribution of female household heads by union status, 1970

Territory	Married	Common-law	Visiting	No longer living with husband	No longer living with common-law partner	Never had husband or common-law partner	Total
	%	%	%	%	%	%	
Jamaica	28.8[1]	17.0	6.3	20.2	26.2	1.6	104 100
Trinidad and Tobago	38.2	11.9	1.8	35.4	11.2	1.5	43 200
Guyana	33.1	8.8	2.3	44.4	10.8	0.7	24 800
Barbados	39.4	16.1	2.6	22.3	17.0	2.6	17 900
Belize	37.7	15.5	3.6	24.5	18.1	0.6	4 700
St Lucia	37.6	16.2	7.5	20.7	17.3	0.7	6 400
Grenada	29.1	19.1	5.0	25.1	20.0	1.8	6 700
St Vincent	34.4	21.1	8.4	10.7	23.0	2.4	5 500
Dominica	31.0	10.5	10.4	24.5	23.2	0.4	4 800
St Kitts/Nevis	37.5	11.1	7.1	18.6	23.8	1.9	3 600
Montserrat	37.8	13.7	3.7	26.3	16.7	1.7	900
British Virgin Islands	43.2	9.7	5.8	18.9	21.2	1.2	500
Cayman Islands	59.5	9.3	0.7	24.5	4.5	1.6	700
Turks and Caicos	56.1	5.0	5.0	28.9	4.0	1.0	400
Mean	32.9	14.8	4.8	26.1	19.9	1.5	224 200
High	59.5	21.1	10.4	44.4	26.2	2.6	
Low	28.8	5.0	0.7	10.7	4.0	0.4	

1. Discrepancies in figures between this table and Table 2 are due to the large number of union statuses 'not stated'.

TABLE 4. Proportional distribution of female and male household heads by educational attainment, 1970

Territory	Male				Female			
	Primary	Secondary	University	Total	Primary	Secondary	University	Total
	%	%	%		%	%	%	
Jamaica	91.2[1]	4.6	2.1	272 300	92.4	4.1	1.0	139 800
Trinidad and Tobago	83.4	11.0	3.0	138 100	89.2	7.4	1.1	50 900
Guyana	87.0	7.7	1.9	99 400	90.7	5.2	0.5	28 700
Barbados	36.5	58.9	3.6	32 900	47.5	51.0	0.7	24 800
Belize	91.3	4.9	2.7	17 200	93.8	4.1	1.1	5 700
St Lucia	92.5	3.3	2.4	12 800	96.6	1.9	0.4	8 900
Grenada	90.5	5.6	2.5	10 400	95.5	3.1	0.3	8 600
St Vincent	91.2	5.2	2.6	9 000	96.8	2.2	0.4	7 500
Dominica	92.2	4.1	2.5	8 700	96.0	2.6	0.5	6 400
St Kitts/Nevis	89.0	4.2	3.5	5 900	93.8	3.1	0.8	5 100
Montserrat	86.5	5.9	6.0	1 800	96.1	1.9	1.3	1 400
British Virgin Islands	75.8	10.3	9.7	1 800	88.6	5.9	3.3	600
Cayman Islands	73.2	9.8	7.4	1 600	89.9	2.6	1.7	900
Turks and Caicos	82.2	6.4	9.4	700	93.2	3.5	2.0	500
Mean	85.7	9.5	2.4	612 600	88.3	8.6	0.6	289 800
High	92.5	58.9	9.7		96.8	51.0	3.3	
Low	36.5	3.3	1.9		47.5	1.9	0.3	

1. Discrepancies in the total percentages are due to omission of the small group 'Other'.

TABLE 5. Proportion of household heads within and outside the labour force, by sex, 1970

Territory	Proportion of household heads in the labour force		Proportion of household heads outside the labour force	
	Male	Female	Male	Female
	%	%	%	%
Jamaica	90.2	47.5	9.8	52.6
Trinidad and Tobago	88.5	33.1	11.6	66.9
Guyana	88.7	32.6	11.3	67.4
Barbados	85.0	46.8	15.0	53.2
Belize	93.3	28.9	6.7	71.1
St Lucia	88.2	42.2	11.8	57.8
Grenada	89.5	46.9	10.5	53.2
St Vincent	88.6	40.2	11.4	60.0
Dominica	88.0	45.5	12.0	54.6
St Kitts/Nevis	86.8	42.4	13.2	57.6
Montserrat	83.4	36.6	16.6	63.4
British Virgin Islands	92.7	46.4	7.3	53.6
Cayman Islands	86.8	35.5	13.2	64.6
Turks and Caicos	87.4	35.9	12.6	64.1
Mean	89.2	42.4	10.8	57.6
High	93.3	47.5	16.6	71.1
Low	83.4	28.9	6.7	52.6

Approximately a quarter of all male household heads in the Caribbean have never been married. This proportion ranges from a high of 45.4 per cent in Jamaica to a low 10.7 per cent in the Caymans. By contrast, Tables 1 and 2 show that almost 50 per cent of female household heads have never been married, ranging from a high 67.3 per cent in St Vincent to a low 29.8 per cent in Guyana. Differences between male and female proportions are relatively large, amounting to as high as 30 percentage points in the case of Montserrat, with the lowest difference being 12.2 percentage points recorded for Trinidad and Tobago.

Caribbean censuses have distinguished between marital status, defined in legal terms, and union status, indicative of the type of relationship existing at the time of the census, in the case of women under age 45, or at age 45, in the case of women 45 years and older. Three types of union are recognized—married, involving legal sanction and co-residence, common law, involving co-residence only, and visiting, indicative of the birth of a child during the year preceding the census although the woman was not in a married or common-law union at the time of the census. Those women who were not in a union, at census time or at age 45, were subdivided into those no longer living with husband, those no longer living with common-law partner, and those who have never had a husband or common-law partner. It is felt that this approach speaks more precisely of the woman's actual involvement than the marital status approach.

On the basis of this approach, Table 3 indicates that in the Caribbean 32.9 per cent of all female heads of household were in married unions in 1970, the largest proportion so far recorded. They are followed, in order of numerical importance, by women not living with their husbands, (26.1 per cent), by women not living with their common-law partners (19.9 per cent) and by women in common-law unions (14.8 per cent). A long way behind come women in visiting unions (4.8 per cent) and women who never had a common-law partner or husband (1.5 per cent).[1] Territorial variations are wide, but this general ordering is maintained throughout the region. There is nothing in the data to indicate the extent to which women in various union types are dependent on their own or their partners' financial resources for their livelihood. According to the census definition the title 'head of household' indicates that the household depends on the person recognized as conducting its affairs, including its economic affairs. Thus, the type of union in which female household heads are involved indicates the possible existence of a supplementary or an alternative source of income to the household. In terms of the given union designations, over half of the women in these households are without such supplementary income originating from the presence of a male in the household.

Unfortunately, union-status data cross-classified with main activity and sex of head are not available at the regional level. However, unpublished data for Barbados reveal a high degree of correlation between union status of female household heads and worker rates of the total female working population according to union status (Spearman's rho = +0.9) [29]. This would seem to imply that women without a resident partner reflect higher worker rates than women with a resident partner.

The degree to which household heads may be expected to discharge their responsibilities may be demonstrated by reference to their level of educational attainment, their involvement in paid employment and their involvement in non-agricultural occupations. It is instructive to examine these characteristics.

Education

Male household heads tend to be better educated than their female counterparts, in that more males tend to proceed to a secondary and

1. These proportions are based on females who head households, excluding 23.9 per cent for whom union status was not stated. If this group is included, the proportions in the union categories decrease but the ordering remains the same.

TABLE 6. Components of estimated labour force of male household heads, 1970

Territory	Worked	Seeking first job	Other seekers	Wanted work and available	Student	Total labour force
	%	%	%	%	%	
Jamaica	91.4	0.3	3.9	4.1	0.2	249 700
Trinidad and Tobago	91.1	1.1	6.9	0.7	0.2	124 400
Guyana	96.5	0.3	1.5	1.5	0.2	88 800
Barbados	98.4	0.1	0.7	0.6	0.1	28 300
Belize	98.2	0.2	0.8	0.6	0.1	16 200
St Lucia	96.6	0.2	2.3	0.6	0.3	11 300
Grenada	98.2	0.3	0.9	0.5	0.1	9 500
St Vincent	96.3	0.3	1.5	0.9	1.2	8 100
Dominica	98.6	0.2	0.7	0.3	0.2	7 700
St Kitts/Nevis	97.7	0.5	0.8	0.7	0.4	5 100
Montserrat	96.2	0.0	1.2	2.3	0.4	1 500
British Virgin Islands	98.9	0.2	0.5	0.4	0.1	1 700
Cayman Islands	98.9	0.2	0.2	0.6	0.1	1 400
Turks and Caicos	95.8	0.6	2.9	0.3	0.5	700
Mean	93.2	0.5	3.7	2.4	0.2	554 400
High	98.9	1.1	6.9	4.1	1.2	
Low	91.1	0.0	0.2	0.3	0.1	

TABLE 7. Components of estimated labour force of female household heads, 1970

Territory	Worked	Seeking first job	Other seekers	Wanted work and available	Student	Total labour force
	%	%	%	%	%	
Jamaica	84.3	1.0	5.4	8.3	0.9	67 100
Trinidad and Tobago	92.5	1.3	5.1	0.8	0.4	17 200
Guyana	95.2	1.0	1.3	1.5	0.9	9 400
Barbados	97.3	0.2	1.0	1.3	0.2	11 700
Belize	98.5	0.4	0.4	0.2	0.5	1 600
St Lucia	94.5	0.7	3.5	0.7	0.7	3 700
Grenada	96.8	0.8	1.6	0.8	0.1	4 100
St Vincent	96.5	0.5	1.7	1.2	0.1	3 100
Dominica	97.1	0.4	1.4	0.8	0.3	2 900
St Kitts/Nevis	96.3	1.0	1.1	0.7	1.0	2 200
Montserrat	94.3	0.0	2.3	3.1	0.4	500
British Virgin Islands	95.3	0.7	0.4	2.9	0.7	300
Cayman Islands	98.1	1.0	0.0	0.3	0.7	300
Turks and Caicos	97.8	0.5	1.6	0.0	0.0	200
Mean	89.3	0.9	4.1	5.0	0.7	124 300
High	98.5	1.3	5.4	8.3	1.0	
Low	84.3	0.0	0.0	0.0	0.0	

TABLE 8. Proportional distribution of household heads by major occupational groups, females, 1970

Territory	Professional and technical	Administrative and executive	Clerical	Sales	Service	Agriculture	Production	Other	Total
	%	%	%	%	%	%	%	%	
Jamaica	7.6	0.2	7.3	15.3	36.0	12.1	15.4	6.1	58 500
Trinidad and Tobago	10.3	0.5	8.7	12.2	36.3	13.9	12.4	5.6	16 200
Guyana	13.2	0.3	6.2	15.5	36.6	16.8	8.8	2.7	9 200
Barbados	5.0	0.4	4.1	16.3	40.2	22.0	8.2	3.8	11 700
Belize	14.0	0.3	4.9	10.2	45.8	8.1	15.2	1.5	1 700
St Lucia	5.0	0.4	5.1	15.3	20.0	38.9	12.0	3.4	3 600
Grenada	4.1	0.3	3.4	9.5	20.2	45.0	14.1	3.3	4 000
St Vincent	5.1	0.1	3.5	9.4	22.7	29.4	14.0	15.8	3 000
Dominica	5.2	0.2	3.5	12.0	22.5	40.7	9.5	6.2	2 900
St Kitts/Nevis	7.3	0.2	4.1	11.3	30.4	38.9	6.0	1.8	2 100
Montserrat	7.1	0.6	4.5	9.6	37.1	33.8	6.1	1.2	500
British Virgin Islands	9.6	1.9	8.4	13.8	58.6	3.1	3.5	1.2	300
Cayman Islands	7.8	1.3	9.5	11.1	59.6	0.3	7.2	3.3	300
Turks and Caicos	12.6	0.6	5.5	9.9	35.7	19.2	13.2	3.3	200
Mean	7.9	0.3	6.6	14.3	34.9	17.4	13.1	5.4	114 200
High	14.0	1.9	9.5	16.3	59.6	45.0	15.4	15.8	
Low	4.1	0.1	3.4	9.4	20.0	0.3	3.5	1.2	

university level of education than females, but the differences between the sexes are marginal. According to Table 4, 85.7 per cent of male household heads in the region and 88.3 per cent of female household heads have attained a level no higher than primary. Among males this range extends from a high 92.5 per cent in St Lucia to a low 36.5 per cent in Barbados. Among females, the range is from 96.8 per cent in St Vincent to 47.5 per cent in Barbados. Differences between males and females at this level range from 16.7 percentage points in the Cayman Islands to 1.2 percentage points in Jamaica in favour of the males. In every territory, the females show higher percentages terminating their education at the primary level. Even in Barbados, which portrays the most favourable education position, the difference is as much as 11 percentage points in favour of the males.

At the secondary level, not much difference is evident. For the fourteen territories, 9.5 per cent of the male household heads and 8.6 per cent of the female household heads have achieved a secondary level of education. At this level, there is much wider territorial variation. Among male household heads, 58.9 per cent attained a secondary level of education in Barbados as compared with 3.3 per cent in St Lucia. Among females, the range is between 51.0 per cent in Barbados and 1.9 per cent in St Lucia and Montserrat. If educational attainment relates to ability to discharge responsibility, it would therefore seem that household heads in Barbados, both male and female, are best equipped in the region to discharge their household affairs.

For the region as a whole, only 2.4 per cent of male household heads and 0.6 per cent of female household heads have achieved a university level of education. Of particular interest is the position of the four largest territories. Barbados shows the highest proportion of its male household heads with diplomas and degrees (3.6 per cent), while the second highest is Trinidad, with 3 per cent. Among female household heads, it is Trinidad that shows the highest proportion with diplomas and degrees (1.1 per cent), while Jamaica is second with 1.0 per cent. Lowest in both cases is Guyana. Among the smaller territories the proportion of female household heads with a university education is consistently less than 1 per cent, except in those territories known to have significant numbers of foreign-born residents, many of whom tend to be professionals.

Employment

It is not proposed to engage in the current debate on the validity of census definitions for permitting an adequate understanding of the meaning of work in the lives of women. Dissatisfaction has been amply

TABLE 9. Proportional distribution of household heads by major occupational groups, males, 1970

Territory	Professional and technical	Administrative and executive	Clerical	Sales	Services	Agriculture	Production	Other	Total
	%	%	%	%	%	%	%	%	
Jamaica	4.4	1.1	2.9	5.2	5.2	43.3	27.9	10.0	232100
Trinidad and Tobago	7.5	2.0	6.1	7.8	7.1	19.2	40.1	10.2	115500
Guyana	6.6	1.3	5.0	5.7	6.9	35.4	28.2	10.9	87400
Barbados	9.3	3.3	4.3	6.9	9.7	18.8	38.1	9.7	27900
Belize	4.9	0.8	3.8	7.0	5.1	41.9	26.2	10.3	15900
St Lucia	3.8	1.5	2.6	3.6	3.9	51.8	29.0	3.7	11000
Grenada	5.8	1.3	3.5	5.4	5.7	41.7	32.4	4.2	9300
St Vincent	4.5	1.7	2.7	6.5	5.0	37.5	29.2	13.0	7800
Dominica	3.7	1.4	2.5	3.0	3.4	55.9	22.8	7.3	7600
St Kitts/Nevis	4.9	1.9	3.4	5.9	5.4	42.3	28.7	7.6	5000
Montserrat	8.1	2.5	2.9	5.9	7.5	28.1	42.8	2.3	1500
British Virgin Islands	10.7	5.3	3.1	4.0	7.5	14.1	48.0	7.4	1700
Cayman Islands	14.9	5.7	3.1	6.8	8.1	7.7	43.4	10.5	1400
Turks and Caicos	11.9	3.0	4.7	4.9	13.2	14.6	44.5	3.3	600
Mean	5.8	1.5	4.1	6.0	6.1	35.3	31.4	9.9	524700
High	14.9	5.7	6.1	7.8	13.2	55.9	48.0	13.0	
Low	3.7	0.8	2.5	3.0	3.4	7.7	22.8	2.3	

TABLE 10. Female proportion in occupational groups of household heads, 1970

Territory	Professional and technical	Administrative and executive	Clerical	Sales	Services	Agriculture	Production	Other
	%	%	%	%	%	%	%	%
Jamaica	0.3029	0.0497	0.3842	0.4250	0.6374	0.0658	0.1224	0.1343
Trinidad and Tobago	0.1619	0.0363	0.1675	0.1801	0.4174	0.0922	0.0416	0.0720
Guyana	0.1750	0.0287	0.1152	0.2248	0.3585	0.0477	0.0318	0.0258
Barbados	0.1844	0.0472	0.2846	0.4976	0.6331	0.3289	0.0823	0.1396
Belize	0.2341	0.0365	0.1228	0.1357	0.4928	0.0204	0.0591	0.0150
St Lucia	0.2983	0.0765	0.3919	0.5801	0.6239	0.1969	0.1190	0.2305
Grenada	0.2355	0.0902	0.2925	0.4347	0.6030	0.3178	0.1581	0.2510
St Vincent	0.3030	0.0226	0.3302	0.3574	0.6373	0.2305	0.1556	0.3177
Dominica	0.3480	0.0614	0.3517	0.6035	0.7159	0.2172	0.1366	0.2452
St Kitts/Nevis	0.3875	0.0404	0.3386	0.4481	0.7057	0.2801	0.0816	0.0929
Montserrat	0.2278	0.0732	0.3433	0.8596	0.4345	0.2886	0.0458	0.1500
British Virgin Islands	0.1214	0.0526	0.2973	0.3495	0.5464	0.0324	0.0109	0.0233
Cayman Islands	0.1048	0.0482	0.4085	0.2677	0.6224	0.0093	0.0355	0.0649
Turks and Caicos	0.2323	0.0500	0.7500	0.3673	0.4362	0.2734	0.0779	0.2222
Mean	0.2296	0.0427	0.2596	0.3434	0.5542	0.0970	0.0834	0.1066
High	0.3875	0.0902	0.7500	0.8596	0.7159	0.3289	0.1581	0.3177
Low	0.1048	0.0226	0.1152	0.1357	0.3585	0.0093	0.0109	0.0150

affirmed in the vast literature on women in development. It is simply proposed to accept that limitations do exist, to proceed on the basis of what is available and to describe very preliminary efforts to supplement the available material with other types.

Attempts to trace movements in the economically active elements of these populations may be made on the basis of data on the main activity of the population during the year preceding the census.[1] Seven categories were identified:

Worked: indicating those persons who were engaged in the production of goods and services for most of the twelve months; this included employers, employees, self-employed workers, unpaid workers.

Seeking first job: covers those persons who spent most of the year seeking their first job.

Others seeking work: includes those persons who have worked previously but who spent most of the year seeking a job.

Wanted work and available: covers those persons who needed a job but who did not spend most of the year job seeking.

Home duties: refers to persons doing household work but receiving no pay.

Student: indicates those persons who spent most of the year in school but had left by the time of the census.

Retired/disabled: covers persons retired for all or most of the year.

From these categories, it is possible to build up estimates of the labour force. This may follow the conventional procedure of workers plus seekers or it may be extended to include students and/or those wanting work and available. Whatever procedure is adopted, the major component of the labour force is undoubtedly the category 'worked'. However, in terms of the number of household heads, over 80 per cent of the males but only 37.9 per cent of the females were recorded as worked. This ranges from the high 45.5 per cent for Barbados to the low 28.4 per cent for Belize. This masks an important distinction which needs to be drawn in terms of membership of the labour force. On the basis of the conventional definition, 89.2 per cent of male household heads are in the labour force as compared with 42.4 per cent of female household heads (Table 5). Within the labour force, however, this wide differential disappears. The largest category within the group is the category 'worked', which accounts for 93.2 per cent of the male and 89.3 per cent of the female elements (Tables 6 and 7). Territorial variation is limited. Among males, the range is from 98.9 per cent in the Caymans and British Virgin Islands to 91.1 per cent in Trinidad. Among females,

1. For discussion on the applicability of labour force concepts in the context of the Caribbean see Roberts [42].

the range is from 98.5 per cent in Belize to 84.3 per cent in Jamaica. In fact, proportions of the labour force who work are markedly similar for male and female household heads.

The second most important category numerically is 'other seekers', which amounts to 40 per cent of the total for each sex. 'Wanted work and available' accounts for 2.4 per cent of the males and 5.0 per cent of the females, while proportions of less than 1 per cent are reported as 'students' and as 'seeking first job'. This reflects the age distribution of the household heads, since the latter two categories tend to consist of young persons who have just left school, very few of whom would be deemed household heads.

Of interest are the categories 'others seeking work' and 'wanted work and available', since these contain elements related to levels of unemployment amongst persons who had previously been employed, an important consideration in respect of those responsible for conducting the affairs of their households. Total unemployment may be taken to include these two categories in addition to 'first-job seekers' and 'students'. According to the estimates built up from these sources, the total unemployment among household heads in the region amounts to 48,000, of which 37,600 or 76.9 per cent consists of males and 13,300 or 23.1 per cent consists of females, which initially suggests extensive unemployment among males. However, in terms of rates, or the proportion of unemployed as a proportion of the labour force, this reflects unemployment rates of 6.8 for males and 10.7 for females in the region. In every category of unemployed, female rates exceed male. Among the males, it is the 'others seeking work' who contribute the most towards unemployment, the rate of Trinidad and Tobago for this group being as high as 6.9 per cent. By contrast, among the females, it is the 'wanted work and available' group that contributes the most, ranging from 8.3 per cent in Jamaica to less than half of 1 per cent in Belize and the Caymans.

Interestingly enough, it is the larger territories that show the highest rates of unemployment. Among male household heads, Trinidad and Tobago shows the highest unemployment rate, 8.9 per cent, as compared with the lowest rate, 1.1 per cent, shown by the Caymans. Among female household heads, it is Jamaica that reveals the remarkably high unemployment rate of 15.7 per cent, followed by Trinidad and Tobago with 7.5 per cent.

Occupation

In terms of their occupational classification, more female household heads are involved in non-agricultural activities than males, except in

Barbados, Montserrat and Turks. According to Table 8 it is the service occupations where the greatest proportion of female heads of households are to be found, one-third of their number being located in this occupational category. Only 8.2 per cent are in professional and administrative jobs, 20.9 per cent in clerical and sales and another 18.5 in production and other occupations. Agricultural activities account for 17.4 per cent, but the range is wide—from 45.0 per cent in Grenada to 0.3 per cent in the Caymans.

Table 9 shows a markedly different distribution for males. Of the 64.7 per cent involved in non-agricultural activities, about one-third are in production, one-tenth in clerical and sales and also in a miscellaneous group consisting mostly of non-agricultural labourers, and 7 per cent in professional and administrative occupations. By contrast agriculture accounts for 35.3 per cent of male household heads. This pattern prevails in virtually every territory.

Two indexes may be derived from these data. The first, presented in Table 10, depicts the proportion of female household heads in each occupational category. This proportion, analogous to Boulding's index of femaleness [3], indicates clearly the extent to which females dominate the service industry, are conspicuous in the sales, clerical and professional occupations and are notably absent from agriculture, production and administrative occupations. Despite some territorial variations, this pattern is evident throughout the region and is probably best depicted by the four larger territories. Among these, the female proportion in service occupations is as high as 0.64 in Jamaica and Barbados, territories with significant sectors of their economy devoted to tourism. But even in Guyana, which records the lowest index among the four (0.36) and indeed the region, this is the occupation that records the highest index among the range of occupational groups covered.

The second index—the index of dissimilarity—uses the approach of Duncan and Duncan [16] and of Gross [20] to measure the extent to which the male (or female) proportional distribution would need to change in order to make the proportional distribution of the two groups identical. [1] For the region, the index amounts to 42, indicating a relatively high degree of occupational dissimilarity between the two sexes. Indexes vary from the high 66 of the British Virgin Islands to the low 22 of Grenada. Those populations that record proportions of over half of the female work force engaged in service occupations, such as the British Virgin Islands and Caymans, register the highest indexes. Those populations in which only about one-fifth of female workers are located in service occupations, e.g. Grenada and St Vincent, register the lowest indexes. Among the remaining territories the indexes range between

1. This index is shown in the last column of Table 1.

30 and 49, indicating fairly extensive sexual differentiation in the occupational composition of the work force of the region.

To summarize then, females account for about one-third of all household heads in the region. They tend to be older and to live alone to a greater extent than men. Their households are approximately the same size as those for men. About half of them live in residential unions, the remainder (46 per cent) either no longer residing with their partner, or participating in a visiting union (4.8 per cent). They tend to be less educated than their male counterparts and to be less engaged in paid employment (including self-employment). Within the labour force, they are as involved in work as males, but the pattern of their occupational distribution is markedly different.[1]

1. No data are available in respect of industry, employment status and hours worked. Data to analyse income differentials are available for both the general population and heads of household. However, the published tabulations combine the categories 'Not stated' and 'None', which together account for over half of all workers, in some cases over 60 per cent. The data are therefore considered suspect and have not been analysed.

3 Strategies for survival

The statistical picture of female-headed households provided by the available census data, limited though it may be by unsatisfactory definitions, nevertheless indicates clearly that women who head households are firmly placed among the disadvantaged sections of Caribbean populations. Because such women tend to be at the bottom of the occupational hierarchy, they tend to reside in the poorest section of the urban areas, in insubstantial and overcrowded housing with inadequate facilities, or, more often, inadequate and shared facilities. Women functioning within such an environment have elaborated a variety of strategies for survival ranging from modification of the household composition, through manipulation of mating partners, friendship and kinship networks to dependence on public welfare. Any one, or any combination of these techniques, provides the woman with a source of livelihood for maintaining the household for which she has ultimate responsibility.

In her study of 'yards' in metropolitan Kingston, Brodber has shown how the main source of emotional and material support for daily problems comes from the communal life provided by the yard [5].[1] Housing units within these yards are rented predominantly by women, many of whom have a semi-resident partner who contributes financially to the upkeep of the unit. Although the partner's contribution is dispensed by the woman, it is nevertheless regarded as the woman's duty to contribute financially to the support of the unit, whether or not the partner actually sleeps in the house. The woman's responsibility there-

1. Brodber uses the term 'yard' to describe a geo-social entity, 'a kind of residential arrangement for low-income Kingstonians', in which women and children form stable units while men drift in and out as the women's circumstances change. Residential units may be rented either from the government (government yards) or from private individuals (tenant yards) [5, p. 9].

fore extends beyond housework and child care to feeding and clothing of dependants, disciplining the children, paying the rent and so on. To assist in the discharge of these responsibilities, the woman cultivates other women in the yard in such areas as child care, child-watching, especially of adolescent girls, sharing household chores, participating in informal credit associations,[1] general companionship, providing sleeping space for the children and so on. In effect, women are able to exploit the communal life offered by a particular form of residential arrangement to assist in the discharge of their own household responsibilities.

Communal residence, however, need not represent the sole source from which women derive assistance. The remainder of this section is devoted to a brief examination of the circumstances of a small group of women who head households and who were part of a pilot study conducted by the Institute of Social and Economic Research (ISER) in connection with a study on the Role of Women in the Caribbean. This study attempts to identify the adaptive strategies employed by women in their role performance in differing life domains, given the changing status of Caribbean women in the context of a rapidly changing socio-economic environment. As part of the study a preliminary questionnaire was administered to twenty-eight women with the aim of testing the feasibility of the proposed questions. The multisectoral questionnaire covered background characteristics, sex-role attitudes, education history and attitudes to schooling, kinship and friendship networks, woman/child relationships, male/female relationships, work activities, and organization and group membership. Of the twenty-eight women interviewed, the circumstances of ten suggest that they are either *de facto* or *de jure* household heads. Relevant information on these ten women follows, with occasional comparisons with the other eighteen women in the group. Of the ten women, six lived in urban areas (two middle-income, four lower-income), the remaining four being resident in lower-income rural areas. Virtually all of them were aged 35 years and over, the mean age being 43.2 years. This corresponds reasonably closely to the census data for 1970, which reveal a median age for female household heads in Barbados of 54.9 years. The small number in the pilot group, the different average used and the heavy weighting with women aged 60 and over would explain some of the difference.

Only one woman was childless, the mean number of children still alive being 3.7, with a range of 1 to 9. No comparable data are available from the 1970 census, but if the mean household size may be used as a proxy, then the figure is the same, 3.7, thus providing a crude estimate of the number of persons for whom the woman is directly responsible.

1. This is known in Jamaica as 'throwing a partner'.

In terms of marital and union status, four of the group had never been married, two were widowed, three were divorced or separated and one was married. Eight of them were not involved in a residential union, although three of those were in a visiting union. Again, this suggests proportions similar to those obtaining with the census data, where 54.3 per cent of the women in female-headed households have never been married and 41.9 per cent were not in a union at the time of the census.

In terms of educational attainment, seven women in the group had not progressed beyond the primary level, and one of these had less than five years of primary schooling. Of the three who progressed to a secondary education, two obtained five GCE 'O' level certificates.

In terms of economic characteristics, six women in the group were engaged in some form of income-earning activity, two in the home and four outside the home. Those engaged in home production activities used handicraft (macramé) and agriculture (vegetables) as their source of earnings. Among those employed outside the home two were employed as domestic workers and two were engaged in professional occupations—one in personnel administration and one in life underwriting. For half of the group their own activity represented their main source of income; two women cited their children and partner as their main sources of income, one cited herself and her partner, but none depended exclusively on the partner. The two widows depended on death benefits or savings left by the deceased husbands. Alternative sources of income seemed to be tapped only in emergencies and then only close kin contributed. None of the women were, or had ever been, on welfare assistance programmes.

The general picture that emerges is one in which members of the household rely on a single female adult, the mother, to provide daily income. For those with generally low levels of education only low-paying manual jobs are possible, thus the need for assistance is evident. Yet none of these women complained about her situation. In fact one even said: 'I have friends who are married and are not as happy as me.'

None of the literature available on women who head households suggests the extent to which unachieved life ambitions may have affected the way in which women develop flexibility in dealing with their social and economic situations. In an early study of peasants in Jamaica, Smith has shown that occupational choices of both males and females undergo significant changes as they move from adolescence to maturity and that the changes correspond with the individual's perception of job availability and the extent of accommodation they are willing to make to close the gap between reality and desire [46]. Girls are seen to be more willing to make accommodations than boys. A more recent study in Trinidad and Tobago has shown how contextual factors such as socio-economic background, ethnic origin, and school status act as constraints on the students' aspirations and how girls tend to have a lower level of occupational choice than boys [11]. The Jamaican study mentioned earlier indicates that girls seem to be more willing to make accommodation to their life situation than boys [46]. It may be argued that skill in dealing with the differences between reality and desire in one domain—occupational choice—may provide skill in dealing with such differences in other domains. The absence of a male in the household in the role of partner/father may be taken to represent another domain in which accommodations between ideal and actual have to be, and are being, made.

The main areas in which females who head households have to make accommodations would seem to be in respect of sources of income, child care, emotional support and self-esteem. Data from the women in the ISER pilot group suggest that the major source of income for these women is their own earning capacity. Their primary concern is to earn, not to satisfy adolescent aspirations. Even so, their responses indicate that the range of occupational choice continues to be limited and to cover traditionally 'feminine' occupations. On leaving school these women wanted to become nurses, teachers, dressmakers, or to work with children, but only one admitted that she 'never did anything about it'. Two women indicated no occupational preference—one wishing to care for her younger brothers and sisters, the other to get married and have children. Only one woman indicated a wish to further her studies—she wanted to study psychology—and she is the only one whose current job involvement is even minimally related to her adolescent ambitions. She is employed in personnel administration.

The second major area in which accommodations have to be made is that of child care. All of the women in the group expressed a preference for caring for their children on their own, but force of circumstances compelled them to seek alternative arrangements. Few of them had the benefit of a non-working mother who could provide that service, and the need for more day nurseries was voiced by at least one respondent.

The institutionalization of child-care arrangements has been identified as one of the critical issues relating to improvements in women's participation in the labour market [34]. This need has been echoed throughout the Caribbean by women's organizations, child-care organizations, welfare departments and on occasion even by government ministers. Such facilities as do exist are provided mainly for preschool children whose parents have to be out at work. Services are provided by both the public and private sector, but no estimates of the number of places provided in the region are currently available. In the government-run day nurseries, staff are required to undergo special training in the care of the young, but this obtains only in the better organized private day nurseries, which in any event tend to be expensive and therefore inaccessible to lower-income persons. There are also a number of individuals who might be termed child-minders, who operate independently but whose activities have been severely criticized. None of the territories operates a system of registered child-minders, such as obtains for example in the United Kingdom.

According to available data (Table 11), the number of day-care centres for pre-school children in the Eastern Caribbean ranges from two in St Kitts and Montserrat to twenty-two in Dominica. Most of them are government-run, but several are privately run, mainly by voluntary organizations with funding from local or regional non-profit organizations and, in two cases, with a government technical-assistance grant.

TABLE 11. Day-care facilities in Barbados and the Eastern Caribbean

	Day nurseries[1]		Pre-schools	
Territory	Government	Private	Government/private	Total
Barbados	15[2]	n.a.	—	15
St Lucia	3	4	—	7
Grenada	2	8	—	10
St Vincent	5	—	—	5
Dominica	1	1	20	22
Antigua	8	—	1	9
St Kitts/Nevis	1	—	1	2
Montserrat	2	—	—	2
TOTAL	37	13	22	72

1. Day nurseries cater to children under 3, pre-schools to those between 3 and 5.
2. Including pre-schools.

These figures do not include the nurseries operated by private individuals. The major users of these facilities are children from households headed by women. In Barbados, such use is not restricted to children from lower-income households but in recent years has been extended to children from middle-income households. But they too are from households headed by women [55].

Day-care facilities for school-age children present particular problems for working parents outside of school hours and during the holidays. None of the territories operates a government scheme to deal with this problem. In some territories private organizations sponsor holiday camps during the summer vacation. The YMCA in Barbados, for example, sponsors two consecutive two-week camps for about sixty children each summer. But this is not a general trend either in Barbados or elsewhere in the region. Moreover, the small numbers involved reflect nothing of the immensity of the problem of providing proper supervision for children during these periods.

One final source of child care lies in the residential establishments operated mainly by voluntary organizations either on their own or in collaboration with government authorities, which provide for orphans, for children who have been abandoned or whose parents are unable to provide proper accommodation and maintenance. Available data from Barbados suggest that while there is a certain amount of short-term care provided, the vast majority of children are in long-term care. Virtually all of the long-term cases are children from female-headed households, the main reasons for their admission being hospitalization of the mother or eviction of mother and children by the mother's current partner (who may or may not be the children's father) [55].

The women of the ISER pilot group have demonstrated that they deal with the problem of child care as need and circumstances dictate. Arrangements range from combining work in the home with child care to the use of female relatives (usually a mother, a grandmother or an aunt) and older children from the home or the neighbourhood to day nurseries and even to taking the children to the work place. One domestic worker who used to take her young children to the home in which she worked reported: 'The people understood. I worked for some nice people. My children had a corner of the house to play in.' Older children of school age are left to fend for themselves after school and during holidays. None of the women were dependent on any of the institutionalized child-care facilities available.

These strategies do not differ from those employed by women who do not head households. One such woman sought a job with flexible working hours that permitted her to be at home at the same time as her children. One gave up her university studies to be at home with her youngest child. Three others preferred to care for their children rather than seek employment or pursue studies. Three women in this group were fortunate enough to be able to afford a maid or nanny to care for their children during their absence at work.

The experience of women in this pilot group suggests that the existence of a need for sufficient and suitable child-care facilities does not prevent women from devising their own strategies to cope with that need. Some of these strategies may not be ideal—such as leaving younger children in the care of older ones, or leaving them unattended, often with tragic results. However, the women recognize their inability to do otherwise and insist that 'there is need for more nurseries here'.

Child care, however, represents only one of the myriad problems that women managing their own households face. The psychological stresses and strains inherent in their double burden of responsibility suggest a need for emotional support, particularly during times of trouble, which a resident partner may have been able to provide. This represents the third major area in which accommodations need to be devised. Recent studies [26, 48, 49, 50] have shown that one of the many positive aspects of the so-called matrifocal family lies in its ability to manipulate a cluster of kin and friendship networks in order to facilitate the discharge of domestic functions. The women in the small group in the ISER pre-test provide tentative evidence of this feature. They appear not to derive emotional and material support from communal residence to the extent that Brodber describes for Jamaica [5]. They do, however draw on near kin, particularly those located near by, to assist with child-care responsibilities. For other kinds of assistance, different strategies are employed. Women in the group differentiated between financial problems for which they sought help from parents, especially mothers, and siblings, and other kinds of problems, for which they turned to other kin, friends and authority figures such as the parson or the doctor. Those women who made no such distinction tended to draw on support from their partner, their baby's father or a good friend, usually a female, but male friends were also cited as reliable sources of support:

> Someone you can rely on and they can rely on you. Someone to talk things over with which they don't repeat. Someone to trust. I prefer male friends. Women don't keep their mouth shut. Men fight and agree again—not women.

Despite the apparent preference for parents, especially the mother, and partners as sources of assistance, it was girl-friends who were most frequently cited as persons to whom the woman turns when problems arise:

> I can ask her to do anything for me and she is always ready and willing. She would do for me first and leave herself out.

> She is a good conversationalist. We help each other financially and otherwise—with work and so.

> She's a good woman, and she has the time because she don't have her own children. I can call on her for help.

Again, women who do not head households do not differ, in terms of alternative sources of support, from women who do. They too draw on kin for immediate practical assistance such as child care, or financial emergencies. But they also tend to look outside the immediate-kin network for other forms of support. Among these women too the sex of the friend is irrelevant: 'He understands me. He is one of the few persons in my life who doesn't pamper me. He tells me like it is.' But it is women friends who tend to figure more prominently:

My employer—she shows a lot of love and understanding. I am like family. She helps me out of my worries.

My girl friend is the person I can discuss my woman-problems with—she tells me her feeling about the trouble I'm having with the children or my man . . . I can talk about my money worries.

In effect, the women in this pilot group appeared to activate lines of exchange and obligation that extended outside the kin network and provided satisfactory levels of emotional support. This appears to be in contradistinction to findings of earlier studies, which have tended to suggest that male peer groups are social units through which males gain recognition and respect [56], while among females dyadic ties tend to be restricted to close kinship and domestic bonds, with extrafamilial relationships being prescribed by formal groups, specifically the church [15]. By contrast, more recent studies have shown that lower-class Creole women maintain closely knit informal relationships, which may or may not develop into formal clubs but which provide a means of adaptation to marginal resources [4] and the development of a sense of solidarity. A study in Montserrat specifically recommends the need for investigation of female friendship networks [35, 36]: 'Who women associate with [other females or males] is important, because it is a way of measuring the degree of alternatives that women have in a culture and the degree to which the sexes are segregated socially; [35, p. 242]. Data from the pilot study do not appear to suggest that women who head households depend on such networks to a greater extent than women who do not. They do suggest that female friendship ties represent an important component in the strategies that women develop for their survival.

Experience with male partners represents the final area to be considered from the perspective of the women in the pilot study, since this may affect the value they place on themselves as individuals. The one married woman in the group of female household heads deemed her marriage unsuccessful because her husband, who was living overseas, 'didn't have enough personality and will-power'. Despite this, she depended on remittances from him to run the household. The one woman in a common-law union considered that her ten-year-old relationship had worked out 'half and half' but had prevented her from migrating as she would have wished. Among the younger single women and those in visiting unions, the theme of independence loomed large. One of them commented: 'Being single fits in with my independent thinking.' Another said of her visiting union: 'I like freedom, so I'm keeping it like it is.'

Women who do not head households are no different in terms of their desire for freedom. One such currently single woman claims: 'You're free. You don't have anybody to dominate over you.' However, older single women, whether or not they run their own households, react to the loneliness caused by the absence of a male partner: 'A distressing state. I never wished it—and when you're older, it's lonely.'

Evidently, regardless of social status and household circumstances, the women in this pilot group were seeking similar qualities in their partners—honesty, companionship, financial support, love, 'total' sharing of life experiences. Some women did find these qualities in past and present partners, but most didn't:

> He was too miserable.
>
> He found a woman who had a lot of money and land and married her.
>
> He was totally selfish.
>
> What [money] he gave was not enough. If I spoke to him about management of money he said it was his money. Yet he didn't want me to work.
>
> His personality and mine didn't mesh.

Yet, unfortunate experiences with partners have not made these women bitter. One of them said, 'I'm happy to be a woman.' Another agreed: 'It's nice to be a woman.' Nor have they made them undervalue their own ability:

> Women are not treated as equals to men, but they are really more than men.
>
> I feel I could compete with any male. If you have the ability to talk and, if you're ambitious, you could push and shove. This should get you through. . . . You learn to understand that women can take more pressures.

The women in this small pilot study represent a variety of life experiences. They do not all originate in lower-income, economically marginal groups; their demographic characteristics are varied; their working patterns are diverse. The only really common feature is that each of them bears sole responsibility for the affairs of her household. While the circumstances that brought this about have varied, the women have all exhibited considerable ability to manipulate their available resources, no matter how slender, in order to provide for their dependants. Despite the many problems they face, none of these women exhibits any desire to be solely dependent on a man. Their attitudes towards men and their own self-images differ little from those of women who share their household responsibilities with male partners.

4 The poorest of the poor

Whether a household is headed by a male or female, the same basic needs of food, clothing and shelter have to be met. The absence of one partner does not necessarily reduce the cost of providing basic services; in fact, costs may well be higher, since they cannot be shared. For example, it may become necessary to pay for certain services that may have been rendered by a partner, such as minor household maintenance and repairs, child care and child-minding. On the other hand, where one partner is functioning as the *de facto* head of the household with little or no assistance from the other, costs are further raised since the non-contributing partner benefits from the available services. Women who bear the sole responsibility for their households have four main sources of income to provide the basic needs of their households: earnings from their own economic activity, maintenance payments for their children, widows' benefits and supplementary benefits.

Supplementary benefits may take the form of national-insurance benefits, allowances permitted on income tax and public assistance. In addition, a range of benefits is provided under the various health and education services. No specific schemes are available for women who head households. They are as eligible for all available benefits as women who do not. Those who support themselves by regular employment can derive benefit from tax allowances and national-insurance benefits. Those who cannot support themselves are forced to rely on public assistance. Regrettably, there are no data to indicate the relative importance of these various sources of supplementary income to women who head households, but available data for one developed country clearly indicates that at least half of the fatherless families rely on supplementary benefits provided by national assistance [12].

A brief description of the principal sources of financial assistance available in Barbados follows.

National-insurance benefits

Sickness benefit is payable to an insured person who is incapable of work through illness. To qualify, an insured person (a) must have been insured for not less than thirteen weeks; (b) must have been employed at the time he/she became ill; or must have not less than thirty-nine contributions paid or credited to his/her account in the contribution year immediately preceding the contribution year in which he/she became ill; (c) must have paid at least eight contributions in the thirteen weeks immediately before the week in which he/she became ill; (d) must produce satisfactory evidence of incapacity for work. The rate of benefit payments varies with the level of weekly earnings and the associated weekly contribution rates. According to the most recently available annual report, that of 1974, women constituted exactly half of all claimants for sickness benefits [2]. However, it is not possible to identify what proportion of the sickness benefit payments went to female claimants.

Maternity benefit is available for specified periods during the pregnancy or confinement of an insured woman and is payable provided that the claimant has paid twenty contributions in the thirty contribution weeks prior to the expected date of confinement. In 1974, a total of Bds$470,844 was paid in maternity benefits to 1,598 claimants, representing $295 per woman for an average of seventy-four benefit days, or approximately $4 per day [2].

Invalidity benefit is offered as a periodical payment of insured persons permanently incapable of work. For most of the period under which the Act has been in operation, high blood pressure and its effects or arthritis have been the major contributors to invalidity.

Old-age contributory benefit is payable to an insured person who has reached pensionable age. Of the 965 claims allowed in 1974, 633, or 66 per cent, were males, and 332, or 34 per cent, were females [2].

Survivors' benefit is payable to a widow and children (under age 16) of an insured person who dies other than by way of employment injury. Where the deceased was a national-insurance pensioner or had title to a pension, a pension is payable to his eligible survivors. Where he had title to an invalidity or old-age grant, the payment takes the form of a lump-sum grant. Pensions are payable for life to widows who are 55 years of age or over and had been married for three years or more at the time of the husband's death. For other widows, the payment is limited to one year, unless they are invalids, in which case payments continue for the duration of the invalidity. Similarly eligible children receive their payments until their sixteenth birthday, except in the case of invalids, who continue to receive their payments beyond age 16. As in all other benefits, the rate of payment depends on the insured person's insurance record. Thus there is no standard weekly rate, as prevails elsewhere. It is, however, noteworthy that of the 116 surviving spouses who received benefits during 1974 three-quarters were over the age of 50 [2]. Thus they were probably receiving additional sources of income. For example, if the widow is a retired worker, she would be receiving an old-age contributory benefit from the National Insurance Scheme and perhaps a pension from her former employer. Further, her deceased husband may have made provisions for her in his will through life insurance and/or other bequests. So that, on the whole, the widow who heads a household is likely to be better off than a woman who has never been married and who heads a household.

Other benefits payable under the National Insurance Scheme include a funeral grant payable on the death of an insured person and an employment injury benefit payable to an insured person for injury or disablement suffered as a result of an injury sustained at the work place.

Tax allowances

Under the existing income-tax regulations, men and women are treated similarly if they are single persons. Individuals may claim personal allowances as follows:

1. Married person whose partner has no income, $3,000.
2. Single person or working spouse, $1,600.
3. For children under 11 years, $400 each; for those between 11 and 16 years educated in Barbados, $500 each; for those over 16 years educated in Barbados, $600 each; those over 16 years educated abroad, $1,000 each.
4. Incapacitated dependent relative not exceeding two income allowances, $500.
5. Other-dependent claim $500.
6. Housekeeper claim $500.
7. Life-insurance premiums: self, $1,500; child under 18, not exceeding $500.
8. Medical expenses: self, $150; children, $75 each.

A number of other allowances on such things as registered retirement plan, covenants, mortgage payments, house-maintenance and repair expenses are also allowed. For a woman who heads a household to benefit from these and all other allowances, she must have regular employment; she must be earning an income of over $6,000 annually. The number of women who fall into this income bracket is probably quite low.

Tax credits

Under the tax-credit scheme recently introduced, persons whose gross income is under $6,000 are credited with an amount equivalent to the tax they would be required to pay on their taxable income. In practice this means that persons with an annual gross income of less than $6,000 do not pay income tax. This applies equally to single and married persons, regardless of sex. Many income-earning women who head households and who fall into this income bracket can benefit from this scheme.

Other benefits

A number of other social-service benefits are available to the population at large, all of which can and do provide help to women who head households:

Educational grants of $100 are available to each child who gains a place in a recognized secondary school on the basis of the Common Entrance (11+) examinations. These grants continue on an annual basis for the duration of the child's secondary-school career.

All places at government secondary schools and the University of the West Indies are provided free of charge.

School meals are provided for all primary schools, milk being included at the nursery schools.

Textbooks are provided free of charge at all primary and government secondary schools.

Medical attention in the form of physical, dental and optical examination and treatment is provided for all schoolchildren mostly free of charge, but in some cases it is subject to an income test. Additionally, adults are eligible for free health care at all the available government health clinics.

Old-age pensions are available to all persons aged 65 and over at the rate of $20 per week. Such persons also receive clothing and food, if necessary, and have their electricity bills and water rates paid by the government.

National assistance

In Barbados, national assistance is available to all needy persons under the National Assistance Act, 1969-37 CAP. 48, the regulations made thereunder in 1969 and subsequent amendment regulations. The National Assistance Act provided for the establishment of a National Assistance Board whose main function is to advise the minister on the provision of assistance to a person who is in need 'by reason of his being prevented by some disability from earning a living, or who has no resources to maintain himself and is unable to find work'. Such assistance is granted to the person designated head of the family on his or her own behalf and for the dependants in the household. According to one of the studies prepared for the National Commission on the Status of Women, of seventy-two cases receiving assistance in two parishes of the island (one rural, the other urban) in 1976, sixty originated from women and, of these, fifty-five were solely responsible for their households [55]. Further, of the sixty women only five lived in a married union. Among the remainder, forty-three were single, seven were separated from their husbands, and five were widowed. The extent to which women who head households rely on national assistance is therefore clearly brought into focus.

How does the system function? General policy is determined by the Ministry of Labour and Community Services and is executed by the Chief Welfare Officer, who is required to discharge the functions of the National Assistance Act in relation to the administration of national assistance. In practice, this is effected by relevant sections of the Welfare Department, which falls within the Ministry of Labour and Community Services. The national assistance section is concerned with the provision of financial assistance according to the regulations laid down by the board. The family-services section attempts to secure financial support from errant fathers for the children of women who apply for national assistance. Such assistance may be in the form of money, food or clothing, or some combination of these. Provision is made in the National Assistance Act for decisions of the Chief Welfare Officer in relation to the administration of national assistance to be reviewed by an appropriate Appeals Committee. This mechanism provides applicants with an opportunity to have their cases reviewed by persons other than government officials.

Under the prevailing regulations, cash grants and assistance in kind may be provided to persons of either sex on the basis of necessity for the duration of need. The current rate for cash grants is $2.50 per week for children under age 16. Children attending school full time are eligible not only for the cash grant but also for school clothing, school fees, spectacles and other necessities. Adults are also eligible for the $2.50 grant, but if they are disabled the grant is increased to $5.00 per week. Women who are unemployed, whose wages are low, who are receiving no child support or whose partners are unemployed are eligible, in addition to the cash grant for themselves and each child, for such items as furniture and clothing where circumstances require.[1] In practice,

1. These conditions are contained in *Laws of Barbados* Public Assistance Act 1969-5.

while the payments are intended to augment income derived from other benefits, including earnings, they often turn out to be the only source of income for the woman and her household. While the selection process is based on a 'most needy' case approach, females, and specifically females who head households, tend to receive more assistance than males. This arises partly because, as one official put it, 'females are more willing to come forward and ask for help, but the males are more hesitant to admit that they need help'.[1] More importantly, however, in situations of chronic unemployment, seasonal employment and low wages, men are finding it increasingly difficult to support their households, or, where they are not resident, their children. Thus women are forced to exploit every available avenue to eke out a livelihood for themselves and their children.

Data from the ISER pilot group suggest that some women who head households may be managing their affairs with a modicum of success, in that they have not been forced to seek financial support from government institutions. Such women are generally those of low to modest income who have struggled with immense problems in order to maintain themselves and their children. Many women, however, are not as fortunate. Available data suggest that, despite their ingenuity, more and more of these women are being forced to rely on public welfare to assist them in their plight. However, the procedures involved in obtaining such assistance have been subject to a number of criticisms. One frequent argument relates to the inordinate delay that often occurs between the request for and the receipt of assistance. Another relates to the inquisitorial procedures involving extensive questioning by one or more public officers. A third relates to the impersonal dispensation of assistance in the welfare offices. It is argued that these factors tend to intimidate prospective seekers and to prevent assistance from reaching where it is most needed.

In Barbados, the process takes from two to four weeks, depending on the woman's circumstances, and involves at least three officers. Initially, a formal application is submitted to the department, either in writing or verbally. A welfare officer visits the household, interviews the applicant and submits a written report to a senior officer who makes the final decision. This may sometimes involve the applicant in another visit to the department. The written decision is mailed to the applicant, who is then required to report to the department, collect a record card from one officer and present it to another, who makes the payment. Where the payment is granted for several weeks, the applicant can spend three or four hours per week simply sitting in a hot, overcrowded and uncomfortable room waiting her turn to be paid. Additionally, where the case

1. Personal communication.

needs to be reviewed periodically, more time has to be spent being interviewed by welfare officers.

The fact that hundreds of women subject themselves to this procedure week after week attests to the severity of their financial circumstances and their utter dependence on what is basically nothing more than a system of poor relief.

Profiles

In order to elaborate further the situation of women who head households, a group of thirty-eight active case-histories of national-assistance recipients were examined. Twenty-seven of the cases were residents in urban areas and eleven in rural areas. Among the urban cases, twenty were *de jure* heads of household, in that there was no resident male partner. Among the remaining seven with resident partners/husband, three partners were chronically ill, one was blind and the remaining three were employed only intermittently. For practical purposes, at least the first four of these could be considered *de facto* heads of household. In the rural areas, only one out of the eleven cases had a resident partner. In terms of marital status, the thirty-eight women studied included four who were married at the time of their first visit to the National Assistance Section, six who were separated from their husbands, and twenty-two who had never been married, four of whom were in a common-law union.

An important demographic aspect of the women who seek national assistance is their age. The average (mean) age at the first visit was 35 among urban women and 32 among rural, with a range of 22 to 64 in the former and 15 to 56 in the latter. This suggests that women are being forced to seek national assistance in what should be the prime years of their working lives. If most women used the scheme during a temporary financial setback there would be no cause for concern. However, the age at which they seek assistance coupled with the length of time for which their cases remain active suggests the need for exploring alternative forms of assistance. Of the thirty-eight cases under review fourteen were active for less than five years, as against twenty-four active for five years or more, and of these, five were active for as many as ten years. The mean duration of time spent on national assistance was 6.1 years. If this is combined with the mean age at entry into the system, it is clear that national assistance has become the main source of livelihood for this group of women. Further, since none of the cases was closed, it is possible that national assistance will continue to remain the main source of support for many years. In effect, the problem of women who head households, who constitute virtually all national-assistance cases, is a long-term one and should be treated as such.

An important indicator of the level of responsibility borne by these women is the number of children under their care. At the first visit, none of the thirty-eight women whose cases were examined was childless, ten had less than three children, eighteen had between three and five children and ten had six or more children. The mean number of children at first visit was 5.0 among urban women and 3.1 among rural women. By the time of the most recent visit, ten women had less than three children, four had between three and five children and twenty-four had six or more children. This gives a mean number of 5.5 children per urban woman and 4.0 per rural woman by the time of the most recent visit. Together these figures imply that a total of 169 children on the first visit and 192 on the last were spending their formative years in an environment affected by the absence of adequate financial support, a lack of proper discipline and a mother who must inevitably be affected psychologically by the stress her disproportionate responsibilities must entail. Further, of the women with three or more children, virtually all were between ages 25 and 44, precisely the ages at which they would be most amenable to training, but the increasing numbers of children and the associated increasing problems make such training virtually impossible.

It has been shown that in the United States, each additional child to a woman who heads a family increases the probability of the family income remaining below the poverty line [51]. This occurs because the woman's prospects for economic independence and security through employment decline with the additional responsibility of more children. This argument holds equally well in poor developing countries like Barbados, where considerable emphasis is placed on education and vocational training as a prerequisite for acceptable forms of employment and where the pattern of 'grandmother' families is no longer dominant.

The available data suggest that households receiving national-assistance benefits rely on those benefits as the principal, in some cases the sole, source of livelihood. At the time of the first visit only three of the thirty-eight women were employed—two in domestic service, one in petty trade—with average weekly earnings of $24. Among the thirty-five who were unemployed at the time of the first visit, ten obtained employment subsequently. Four were domestic service workers, four agricultural labourers and two were employed as cottage workers doing smocking for the garment industry. The average weekly earning was $26 in the urban areas and $36 in the rural areas. None of the thirty-eight, except the thirteen who were employed for brief periods, were able to supplement the national-assistance benefit by personal earnings.

The evidently limited availability of financial resources raises the question of alternative support. One possible clue may lie in the household structure, in that the presence of adults may represent a potential source of additional income. Of the thirty-eight cases, ten consisted of the woman and her children alone, while nine included a resident partner. A further fourteen cases consisted of three-generational households comprising grandmother, mother and children; four cases were laterally extended structures in that they consisted of a woman and her children, her sister(s) and/or brother(s) with their children, and one case included a woman, her children and her maternal aunt. In effect, two-thirds of the households contain at least one other adult member from whom a financial contribution should theoretically be available. In practice, however, this is far from the case. In the three-generation households the grandmother contributes either by virtue of her ownership of the house, which is often in a dilapidated condition, by paying the house rent, if she is employed, or by giving her pension to the younger woman. In the four laterally extended households, one sister was able to contribute by paying the house rent and another was the sole source of support. The others were either unemployed or of school age. In the nine households with a resident partner, four partners were ill (one mentally ill, one blind and two incapacitated), five were employed intermittently and contributed when they could, one owned the house in which the couple lived, but provided nothing else. Among the remaining households, assistance came from occasional child-support payments, from grown-up children who contributed when able, and from friends.

Altogether, each of the thirty-eight households contained an average of about 2.5 adults, of which an average of less than one provided some form of income contribution, and that only occasionally. In the rural areas, the non-contributing household members tended to be mothers and grandmothers and to a lesser extent aunts, that is persons of relatively advanced age whose ability to contribute would be minimal. In the urban areas, the non-contributory household members tended to be unemployed sisters, daughters and partners. The main contributors in both types of areas were sons, partners and brothers, all of them doing so only when economic circumstances permitted. The distinguishing characteristic of the cases studied is that they originated in households characterized by the absence of a main income-earner and that even where two or more earners were present employment was intermittent and concentrated in the low-skill, low-paying occupations. Thus none of the households could be classified as having a steady source of income, and reliance on national assistance could be expected to continue.

Another potential source of income lies in child-support payments from fathers of children. The number of fathers responsible for the 169 children dependent on the thirty-eight women was seventy-six; thus there was an average of two fathers per household, with a range of one to seven. Presumably, if each father contributed to his child(ren) at the prevailing rate of $10 per week, the household income would average at least $40 per week. If the woman was employed, even at a minimum wage, welfare assistance could then be used as a temporary relief measure. It has been argued that, on the basis of this line of reasoning, many women deliberately cultivate a series of partners with the specific intention of collecting several support payments. In this way, they can be assured of a steady income without themselves having to be engaged in economic activity. Fathers, however, do not appear to contribute with any degree of regularity, if they contribute at all. Of the seventy-six men involved, twenty-one provided support of some kind as they were able. Another twenty-six provided no support, either because they refused to do so, their whereabouts were unknown or they preferred to go to gaol rather than honour a court order. Another fourteen had migrated, nine were deceased and six were ill, five of them mentally. Once again, another possible source of income proves chimerical.

In the Appendix to this book six case histories are outlined that highlight the differing kinds of situations that force women to assume total responsibility for their households and force them to rely on social welfare as an important and in some instances the only source of income.[1] All of the cases originated in low-income areas within the main urban parish. All of the women were relatively young, being between 25 and 34 on the first visit; all of them had more than three children; all of them were unemployed at the time of their first visit, though two were able to find employment later on. In two of the six cases (numbers I and II), there was a resident male, but both of them worked intermittently, and in one case no sooner was regular employment obtained than the man was crippled by permanent illness (Case II). In another, minimal assistance was provided by persons outside the household, a mother and the father of one child (Case V). In all cases it was the women who made the request for assistance and in all cases it was evident that the household depended for its existence on the woman's ingenuity. In only one case was the household on welfare for less than five years (Case V), one case being on the books for as many as nine years (Case I). In no case did the circumstances suggest that it was reasonable to expect a cessation of welfare in the short term. The case reviews therefore serve to validate the distinction drawn by Buvinić and Youssef between *de jure* and *de facto* heads of household [9]. They also support the census data findings in respect of employment among these women.

The main problems faced by the women cited in these cases have

1. Assistance provided by the Welfare Department in compiling these case-studies is gratefully acknowledged.

been monetary, but other cases reveal other problems. Housing conditions, for example, are revealed to be poor and substandard. In some cases the Welfare Department finances the repair of the house or in others it recommends the case to the Housing Authority for provision of public housing. Recently the department has established an internal Housing Unit that seeks to deal with housing problems more quickly. Another critical problem area relates to the care and supervision of children. In cases where the single (female) parent is employed, and no other adult lives in the household, it is not uncommon for older children to be kept at home to care for pre-school children, or even for the young ones to be left unsupervised in the home [55]. Alternative arrangements include child-minders in the immediate neighbourhood, privately run nurseries that are very costly, or day-care centres operated by the government-subsidized Child Care Board. Fees at these centres are placed at $2.50 per week and the majority of children using the facilities are drawn from female-headed households [55]. But even with this range of facilities the problem of supervision of children during the mothers' working hours remains critical.

Several factors appear to have contributed to the circumstances of these households. Essentially, it was a combination of unemployment (Case VI), intermittent employment (Cases I and II), low wages (Case II), large numbers of children, i.e. six or more, (Cases III and V), emigration of male partner (Case III), ill health (Cases II and III), unscrupulous male partners (Case IV) and perhaps even sheer bad luck (Case II). Evidently, the quantum of assistance in cash is abysmally low, but in poor countries, where a little has to be spread a long way, it is hardly likely that a more attractive grant can be offered. Where, however, the grant is supplemented by other assistance, such as shoes and clothing, it cannot be denied that some help is available. Further, in the case of old persons living alone, who receive not only old-age pensions, but also clothing, food, daily hot meals, in some cases, and payment of water rates and electricity bills, there can be no doubt that at least some of the needs of these women are being met.

The question of child-support payments raises rather different issues. According to the present laws of Barbados, the court is authorized to order the payment of a fixed sum—a maximum of $30 per week for the wife and $10 per week each for all children under 16 years of age—and in default to impose the remedy of distress or the penalty of imprisonment.[1] The wife forfeits her right to this entitlement on evidence of adultery; however, the entitlement of the children of the marriage is preserved. For women in other unions, no such support

1. *Laws of Barbados*. Married Women (Separation and Maintenance) Amendment Act, 1977–74.

obligation is provided by law. What is possible, through the Affiliation Act, is an affiliation order in favour of the children, provided satisfactory evidence of the child's paternity is established. The woman has no legal claim to financial assistance [18].

In both cases, the procedural requirements necessary both to fix the maintenance payment and to secure that payment are regarded as unduly restrictive. The National Commission on the Status of Women felt that the principle of a fixed maximum is unsatisfactory, since in many cases orders are known not to reflect either the magnitude of the problem or the ability of the partner to pay [55]. For example, data for the years 1975 and 1976 indicate that of a total of 1,008 orders 873 related to affiliation cases and 135 to married women's cases. Neither figure is regarded as a true reflection of the extent to which women need this source of income. In the case of married women, for example, although the divorce courts represent a viable alternative, the legal fees are so prohibitive that women prefer to seek a magistrate's court order for maintenance or not to use the courts at all.

Evidence from a variety of sources suggests that considerable difficulty obtains first in the enforcement and collection of court orders [14, 24, 55]. In Barbados high rates of default have been reported: 'Some men, besides shirking their full responsibility of parenthood, allow arrears to accumulate and seem to prefer to go to prison in default of payment' [55, p. 684]. In one of the cases examined for this study, one father even threatened to kill the woman if she sought a court order against him for the support of his child. In an attempt to deal with this problem the National Commission on the Status of Women recommended that enforcement procedures be reviewed and attachment of earnings be introduced (Recommendation No. 16), that the application of a fixed sum for maintenance be abolished (Recommendation No. 14), and that a means test be applied before affiliation and maintenance orders are adjudicated (Recommendation No. 168). Although steps are being taken to implement Recommendation No. 16, nothing has been done so far about either Recommendation No. 14 or Recommendation No. 168.

In Jamaica, the only territory so far to establish a Family Court, orders are made according to the discretion of the judge. A means test may be instituted by the Probation Department on the recommendation of the judge, and children must be supported up to the age of 16, or if deemed necessary to the age of 18. The problem of non-compliance with court orders has been tackled by the implementation of attachment orders, which permit routine deduction from the father's income, collection by specially designated court officers and the issuance of a warrant of distress if the allowance falls into arrears [24]. Despite these laudable efforts, the major constraint on child-support collection efforts in these territories is the location of the errant fathers. In situations where mobility within the country is so easy, where emigration out of the country is so prevalent and where some men simply prefer to go to prison rather than settle child-support payments, the problem becomes intensified and the plight of women and children dependent on those payments becomes that much more unfortunate.

5 Conclusion

The region from which the data presented in this paper originate represents one of the world regions that have been described as being at an intermediate level of economic development—the so-called 'middle-income nations'. One of the territories, Jamaica, has even been placed in the upper middle-income category of this intermediate range on the strength of per capita income in excess of $1,075 in 1975, a level that markedly exceeds those prevailing for many countries in Asia, Africa and Latin America. According to the World Bank, gross domestic product per capita income ranged from $1,131 in Jamaica to $335 in Grenada in 1974 [10]. This masks a considerable amount of internal variation. In order to illustrate the degree of poverty prevailing in the region, the World Bank has developed a Food Working Days Index, which indicates the number of days that a person in the occupational category showing the lowest mean wage in each territory would have had to work in the period June–August 1973 to buy a basket of basic goods. The proportion of the working population concentrated in the lowest-paid categories is used as an indicator of the extent of poverty [10]. On this basis, indexes of the degree of poverty are seen to range from 7.72 in St Kitts/Nevis to 2.08 in Jamaica in 1973, with a mean for the region of 3.61. The index of the extent of poverty ranges from 54.0 in Jamaica to 10.2 in Antigua in 1970, with a mean for the region of 35.5. From this it is evident that the region is undoubtedly a poor one and that along with poverty, unemployment and inequality of income must also rank as the major economic problems of the region. And, as elsewhere in the Third World, it is on women that these problems impinge most heavily [1].

One of the groups most readily identifiable and most vulnerable to poverty is that group of women who head households. Such women retain prime responsibility for child care, sometimes care of other adults, home maintenance and income earning on behalf of other household members.

Women in the Caribbean have been socialized essentially for parental, conjugal and domestic roles, but historically have been associated with considerable occupational role performance. The success with which they have manipulated their occupational roles has in part been related to their level of formal education and vocational training, the availability of job employment opportunities and the level of earnings available. More important, it has been related to their ability to manipulate such personal resources as they may possess in order to exploit the available income-earning possibilities. Allied to this is their ability to combine income-earning activities, whether within or outside the home, with household responsibility. An extended family structure provides the woman with access to a source of child care and home-maintenance support and permits her to experiment with alternative economic-support strategies. This partially explains the ability of rural and urban lower-income women to control the local fruit and vegetable section of the distributive sector for many years. The modernization process of Caribbean economies over the past twenty or thirty years, with its highly visible focus on imported technology, specialized enterprises and individualistic philosophy, has served to undercut women in the one area in which they had attained predominance. Thus, although women are still found in large numbers in the informal sector, few of them retain prominence in the local food-distribution chain. Instead they are to be found as petty traders lining the streets of the major towns and subject, to an even greater extent than the big merchants, to the vicissitudes of the international monetary economy. At the same time the decline of the extended family has brought to the forefront the problem of combining income-earning and home-maintenance activities. For women who head households this represents a crucial consideration.

The data analysed in the earlier sections of this book not only provide some insights into the characteristics and coping strategies of females who head households but also identify poverty as the major problem of such households. The census data indicate clearly that women who head households are concentrated in low-paid, low-status occupations with no prospects for improvement. They are more likely to be unemployed than their male counterparts, more likely to be involved in low-paying occupations and more likely to be untrained for any occupation at all. The data from the ISER study suggest that, regardless of income-earning level and socio-economic background, women who head households face similar problems, the most critical of which appears to be related to sources of livelihood and child-care obligations. As in many other countries, these women depend to a large extent on the creation of network alliances that permit reciprocal arrangements with other females for child care, household duties, food or cash in emergency situations and general emotional support [25, 38, 40].

The welfare data indicate that recipients of national-assistance grants are overwhelmingly women who are *de facto* heads of households, virtually all of whom are unemployed. Theirs is the problem of poverty. Presumably, if such women were employed in similar occupations and received similar incomes to those of men they would be exposed to less poverty and less dependence on welfare. This point has been argued for both developed [31, 32, 45, 51] and developing countries [44]. The tragedy of these women is that no immediate solution appears imminent. Discontinuance of welfare assistance is clearly an untenable proposition, since the earning strategies employed by the women have not been markedly successful.

The first strategy that seems to be attempted is that of seeking employment. Younger women may find employment in the commercial, manufacturing and service industries. But unless they are well educated, such employment tends to be short term. Older women, who are unlikely to have any occupational training, attempt a range of activities such as washing, ironing, cleaning, casual labour and petty trade. Invariably, such activities also tend to be short term. Further, unanticipated changes in the household arrangements, such as the ill health of parent, the birth of baby, eviction, might require immediate attention to the exclusion of wage-earning activity.

Another strategy appears to be multi-partnering. In the Dominican Republic, it has been represented that multiple serial mating indicates the presence of a flexible male network that not only functions as a nuclear family but affords the woman food, shelter, 'reproductive success' and psychological satisfaction [6, 7]. By contrast a study in Brazil suggests that this strategy is not always successful [33]. The pilot-study data in the present book suggest that the practice is regarded with disapproval: 'I don't like the idea of moving in with a man and having to move out, then moving in with another. . . . I don't believe in having children from different men.' The welfare data suggest that if multi-partnering is being used as a coping strategy it is singularly unsuccessful. Both past and present partners are contributing either nothing or very little to the woman's household, even if they have fathered some of her children. Some of this may be attributable to unscrupulous males, but much appears to be related to the constraints on employment and earning possibilities for males, which severely limit their ability to contribute to the household. Migration, absconding and gaol may well represent rational alternatives to shame and embarrassment.

Another type of strategy appears to be reliance on other members of the household. Data not used in this paper suggest that in the Caribbean dependence on children as economic supporters is not widespread, owing to the great value attached to schooling. Thus households can only derive some benefit from wage-earning children when those children leave school. And then they are likely to be either unemployed or earning low levels of income that provide only marginal assistance, if it is offered to the household at all. Other adults in the household tend to be beyond the prime working age, and to be female rather than male; thus they too face the same constraints in terms of job opportunities as the head of the household. With little or no supplementary earnings from other members of the household, the woman responsible for the household is then forced to turn to the welfare system as a valid economic option for the survival of her household. Alternative sources of assistance may exist, but the data do not identify these and, in the case of the welfare data, there is little evidence that such sources are actively sought. A heavy burden is thus placed on meagre welfare sources of basically impoverished societies.

One of the deficiencies of national statistical infrastructures in the region is the inability to provide what may be construed as estimates of a poverty threshold. It is therefore not possible to indicate the proportion of female-headed households currently existing below such a line. What is evident is that those who depend exclusively on welfare payments to compensate for lack of an earned income by the woman or lack of child-support payments do exist at levels well below a minimally acceptable level of living, however that is defined. Prevailing welfare payments are patently incapable of providing economic security to the woman and her household. Yet they are crucial to their existence.

Although the need for welfare provisions is recognized, the relationship between welfare assistance and female-headed households is by no means straightforward. It may be that increasing numbers of female household heads have forced authorities to devise welfare-assistance programmes of a particular type. By contrast, it may also be that the continual availability of institutional support of the kind provided by welfare programmes acts to encourage the establishment of female household heads. Case V, for example, seems to suggest this. If the latter is the case, then the need for a reassessment of existing programmes and reformulation of policy becomes evident. The choice for Caribbean societies would seem to be that between programmes designed to sustain and those designed to rehabilitate. In the latter regard planners need to emphasize policies that include skill-acquisition, income-generating and adult-education programmes, for both males and females. The general aim of such programmes should be to provide poor households not only with basic necessities but also with the motivation and the capacity for self-improvement. Policies directed towards males should be aimed at providing them with an economic resource base that could equip them to fulfil their household responsibilities. Policies directed towards females should aim at:

Devising income-generating programmes that not only permit women to work from within the household but provide them with the physical and capital assets required to do so.

Ensuring that employment-creating programmes contain a component designed specifically for women.

Providing institutionally supported child-care centres operating at times convenient to the women's work schedules.

Expanding the opportunities for part-time work.

Increasing opportunities for furthering formal education and for receiving technical training.

It is important that the programmes designed to execute such policies are not restricted to traditional approaches. By providing technical training in non-traditional areas, by arranging with employers and trade unions appropriate conditions of work for part-time workers and by organizing certain kinds of work on a cottage-industry basis, it is immediately possible to provide older women with a wider range of occupational choices. By expanding the notion of day-care services to include such options as day fostering, registered child-minders, employers' day nurseries, combination day nurseries and play groups, and home help for the care of the elderly, it is immediately possible to provide a safe environment for the dependants of women who head households, during the time they are at work. By including, in programmes for adult education, arrangements for the release from work of early school-leavers in order to permit them to complete their education, it is possible to equip young men and women for participation in the job market. These proposals are based not only on an evaluation of the situation but also on the observations of women themselves. The women in the pilot study were asked: 'What kinds of projects for women would you like to see organizations introduce in your area?' Their responses are instructive:

I would like to see them get together any talent that can be used to help in any way. They could form groups not only for selling but also in a charitable way. They should try to give younger people more understanding about parenthood and so on. They could come together in a group, make things and get them sold . . . to raise funds. It can help if one week one person can't pay the rent. The theme would have to be: 'Love you one another.'

I would like to see these organizations give women help so they can take mothers and teach them different things like providing things for children which they couldn't provide.

Poor women should have people come into their community rather than the women going out. You would be able to look after your children if people come in to you.

I would like to see these organizations help the women to get employment when they are finished being involved in a particular project.

I would like those organizations to start uplifting woman the same way they used to preach that man is more than woman.

The dominant themes in these statements provide the basis for a comprehensive policy programme—self-fulfilment, skill-training, job-creation, child care—flexible programme schedules, adult education, especially for the younger people, community co-operation. By treating these proposals as an integrated package guided by the expressed concerns of the women affected rather than a loose and fragmented collection of programmes, it is possible to assist women who currently face the problem of managing their households single-handed to equip younger women to cope with that problem if it arises later in their lives and maybe even to reduce the rising incidence of this phenomenon.

Appendix

Six case-studies of welfare recipients

The following accounts are based on actual cases, but fictitious names are used for obvious reasons.

Simple family household:
woman, common-law partner and her children

Case I: Vashti was 30 years old when she first applied for assistance in 1970. At the time her marital status was single, but she lived in a common-law union with the father of four of her five children. The father of her eldest child had emigrated, and she received no support from him for his child. The father of the other children was occasionally employed as a 'lorry hand', during which periods he contributed $25 per week. Vashti herself was unemployed with no prospects of employment, and all her children were at school. She applied for monetary assistance and educational assistance for the children. She was granted school uniforms for two of the children and $5 per week.

Three years later, Vashti made her second application. By this time she had two more children and one baby who had just died. She requested and was granted funds to bury the baby.

In 1979, Vashti had returned to the department. During the interval she had had two more children—making a total of nine—and her common-law partner had just been sentenced to four and a half years in prison. She had been occasionally employed as an agricultural labourer but was then unemployed. She requested financial assistance and was granted $15 per week. Two months later she requested assistance for the children and received school uniforms.

Case II: Eudine, aged 28, first applied in 1974. At that time, her marital status was single but she lived in a common-law union with the father of her three children. During her last pregnancy she had resigned from her job in a garment factory, and she was still unemployed. Her partner made and sold souvenirs during the tourist season, thus his financial contribution to the household was limited. The household consisted of Eudine, her common-law partner, their children and his mother. Her first request was for financial assistance, which she received.

By the next year, Eudine's partner had obtained a job as a chauffeur that paid $30 per week. Eudine requested and received school uniforms and shoes for the children. Four months later she requested a mattress and received both bed and mattress.

In 1976 and 1977 educational assistance was again granted. By 1978, when Eudine's case was reviewed, it appeared that her circumstances had improved. The couple had married and both of them were working. The financial assistance provided over the years was therefore terminated.

By 1979 Eudine had re-applied. By this time she had had a fourth child, but her husband had suffered a stroke and the prognosis was that he would be unlikely ever to work again. Eudine's wage as a domestic of $60 per week was unable to cover the family's expenses. Financial assistance was received and school uniforms provided for the children.

Truncated simple family household: woman and her children

Case III: Joan was 33 years old when she first applied for assistance in 1977. Separated from her husband for three years, she was the mother of six children. The father of the first had migrated, the father of the other five, her husband, was an outpatient of the mental hospital and therefore unable to offer any contribution. She was unemployed. The household consisted of Joan, her six children and her common-law partner, who had asked her to leave his house. She requested financial assistance for the children and was granted $12.50 plus emergency supplies of a bed and mattress, stove, chairs, linen, cooking utensils, crockery, cutlery and foodstuff. Within six months she applied for and received school uniforms for the children and again in 1978.

In 1979, Joan was injured in a vehicular accident and applied for disability aid, which she received—$8 per week. Later in the year, she made two further applications, one for educational assistance, another for bed linen. Both were granted.

In March 1980, Joan applied for a food voucher, which was granted, and in April for a stove and oven. That also was granted.

Over a period of three years, for the whole of which time she was entirely responsible for herself and her children, Joan was forced to seek welfare assistance on seven occasions.

Case IV: Daphne first applied in 1974 at the age of 29. She was separated from her husband and had five children. The father of the first child offered no assistance, while her husband, the father of the remaining four children, was currently serving time in prison for refusing to support his children. The household consisted of Daphne and her five children, who lived in a house for which the rental was $12.50 per week. On her first application, she requested financial assistance for herself and children and received $12.50 for the children and school uniforms for her eldest child.

Between 1974 and 1979, Daphne had made six other applications, all of which, except that for housing, were granted. The request for housing is still pending. During the period Daphne's husband had been released from prison but could not be located.

Laterally extended family household: woman and her children, her sister and her children

Case V: Nesta was 27 years old on her first application in 1975. Her marital status was single; she was not in a residential union. She had had seven children by five men, of whom two gave no assistance, one was unemployed, one was dead and one gave $5 per week for his child. Nesta normally worked as a domestic, but had chosen to remain at home to care for the children. The household consisted of Nesta and her seven children and Pearly, Nesta's sister, and her eight children. Pearly was also unemployed. The main source of financial assistance came from the father of Pearly's children, who was not resident in the household, and the sisters' mother, who worked as a domestic and who was also not resident in the household. On her first application Nesta requested financial assistance for the two children whose father was dead. She received $15 per week for six of the seven children—the one whose father supported it was excluded.

Within four months Nesta made her second application, this time for clothing and shoes for five of the children. This was granted. Similar requests were made and granted in 1976, 1977, 1978 and 1979. In reviewing this case in 1978, the officer noted Nesta's uninterested attitude to seeking employment, and complaints from Pearly and their mother about Nesta's attitude (by this time Pearly was working).

Over a period of four years Nesta made seven applications, all of which were approved.

Woman, her children and her brother's children

Case VI: Mabel first applied in 1974, when she was 25 years old. She was single, not in a union and had three children, the father of whom was deceased. She had previously been employed as an electronic assembler, but had been laid off two months previously. The household consisted of Mabel, her three children and Mabel's sister, who paid the rent. Mabel requested and received financial assistance—$5 per week. In 1975 and 1976 she applied for educational assistance for the children and received school uniforms. An application for a mattress and sheets was apparently turned down.

In 1977, Mabel's household increased. Her brother had killed his wife, who had four children, and he was sentenced to life imprisonment. Mabel offered to care for three of the brother's children. Her next three applications—1977, 1978 and 1979—were therefore in respect of education assistance for six children, her three and her brother's three. All six children were provided with school uniforms and, on the last occasion, financial assistance.

References

1. ANTROBUS, Peggy. Promoting and Accelerating Women's Participation in Developing Programmes in the Caribbean through TCDC. Paper prepared for UNDP High-level Meeting on the Review of TCDC, January 1981.
2. BARBADOS. NATIONAL INSURANCE BOARD. *Report on the National Insurance and Social Security Scheme for the Period January 1, 1974–December 31, 1974*. Mimeo. n.d.
3. BOULDING, E. et al. *Handbook of International Data on Women*. New York, Wiley, 1976.
4. BRANA-SHUTE, Rosemary. Women, Clubs and Politics: the Case of a Lower-class Neighbourhood in Paramaribo, Suriname. *Urban Anthropology*, Vol. 5, No. 2, 1976, pp. 157–85.
5. BRODBER, Erna. *A Study of Yards in the City of Kingston*. Kingston, Jamaica, ISER, UWI, 1975. (ISER Working Paper No. 9.)
6. BROWN, Susan. Love Unites Them and Hunger Separates Them: Poor Women in the Dominican Republic. In: R. Reiter (ed.), *Toward an Anthropology of Women*. New York, Monthly Review Press, 1975.
7. ——. Lower Economic Sector Female Mating Problems in the Dominican Republic: A Comparative Analysis. In: R. Rohilich-Leavitt (ed.), *Women Cross Culturally: Change and Challenge*. The Hague, Mouton, 1975.
8. BUVINIĆ, M. et al. *Women Headed Households: the Ignored Factor in Development Planning*. Washington, D.C., International Centre for Research on Women, 1978.
9. BUVINIĆ, M.; YOUSSEF, N. Households Headed by Women in Third World Countries: an Overview. Paper presented to ICRW Conference on Women in Poverty: What Do We Know? Belmont Conference Centre, Elkridge, Maryland, 30 April–2 May 1978.
10. CHERNICK, S. E. *The Commonwealth Caribbean: The Integration Experience*. Baltimore, published for the World Bank by the Johns Hopkins Press, 1978.
11. COLE, Joyce. Occupational Choice of Fifth Form Students in Trinidad and Tobago. *Bulletin of Eastern Caribbean Affairs*, Vol. 3, Nos. 5, 6, 1977, pp. 12–16.
12. COMMITTEE ON ONE-PARENT FAMILIES (UNITED KINGDOM). *Report.* Vols. I, II, Cmnd. 5629. London, HMSO, 1974.
13. CUMPER, G. E. The Jamaican Family: Village and Estate. *SES*, Vol. 7, No. 1, 1958, pp. 76–108.
14. CUMPER, Gloria. *Survey of Social Legislation in Jamaica.* Kingston, ISER, UWI, 1972.

15. DIRKS, R. Networks, Groups and Adaptation in an Afro-Caribbean Community. *Man*, Vol. 7, No. 4, 1972, pp. 565–85.
16. DUNCAN, O. D.; DUNCAN, B. Residential Distribution and Occupational Stratification. *American Journal of Sociology*, Vol. 60, No. 5, 1955, pp. 493–503.
17. FORDE, Norma. Divorce. In: Barbados, National Commission on the Status of Women, *Report*, Vol. 2, pp. 277–99. Bridgetown, Ministry of the Attorney General, 1978.
18. ——. Maintenance. In: Barbados, NCSW, *Report*, Vol. 2, pp. 271–6. Bridgetown, Ministry of the Attorney General, 1978.
19. GREENFIELD, S. Dominance, Focality and the Characterisation of Domestic Groups: Some Reflections on 'Matrifocality' in the Caribbean. In: S. N. Gerber (ed.), *The Family in the Caribbean*, pp. 31–49. Rio Piedras, University of Puerto Rico, Institute of Caribbean Studies, 1973.
20. GROSS, E. Plus ça change . . . ? The Sexual Structure of Occupations over Time. *Social Problems*, Vol. 16, Fall 1968, pp. 198–208.
21. HARRIS, Olivia. Households and Household Heads: A Critique of the Domestic Mode of Production. Resource paper sent to IDS/CEREP Seminar on Women and Social Production in the Caribbean, San Juan, 23 June–25 July 1980.
22. HIGMAN, B. W. The Slave Family and Household in the British West Indies, 1800–1834. *Journal of Interdisciplinary History*, Vol. 6, No. 2, Autumn 1975, pp. 261–87.
23. HOROWITZ, Michael M. *Morne Paysan: Peasant Village in Martinique*. New York, Holt, Rinehart & Winston, 1967.
24. JACKSON, Jean. Stresses Affecting Women and Their Families. Paper presented at ISER Workshop on the Women in the Caribbean Project, September, 1980. Mimeo.
25. KOUSSOUDJI, Sherrie; MUELLER, Eva. The Economic and Demographic States of Female Headed Households in Rural Botswana. Mimeo, n.d.
26. LADNER, Joyce. *Tomorrow's Tomorrow: the Black Woman*. New York, Doubleday, 1971.
27. LASLETT, P. *Household and Family in Past Time*. Cambridge, Cambridge University Press, 1972.
28. MASSIAH, Joycelin. Indicators of Women in Development: a Preliminary Framework for the Caribbean. Paper presented to Unesco Meeting of Experts on the Indicators of the Extent of Women's Participation in Socio-Economic Development, Paris, 21–24 April 1980.
29. ——. Women in Barbados: Some Demographic Aspects of their Employment. In: Barbados National Commission on the Status of Women, *Report*, Vol. I, pp. 100–204. Bridgetown, Ministry of the Attorney General, 1978.
30. ——. *Women in the Caribbean: An Annotated Bibliography*. Cave Hill, Barbados, Institute of Social and Economic Research, UWI, 1979.
31. MCEADDY, Beverley Johnson. Women Who Head Families: a Socio-Economic Analysis. *Monthly Labor Review*, Vol. 99, No. 6, 1976, pp. 3–9.
32. ——. Women Who Head Families, 1970–1977: Their Numbers Rose, Income Lagged. *Monthly Labor Review*, Vol. 101, No. 2, 1978, pp. 32–7.
33. MERRICK, T. W.; SCHMINK, Marianne. Households Headed by Women and Urban Poverty in Brazil. Paper presented to ICRW Conference on Women in Poverty: What Do We Know? Belmont Conference Centre, Elkridge, Maryland, 30 April–2 May 1978.
34. MOORE, Kristin; SAWHILL, Isabel. Implications of Women's Employment for Home and Family Life. Paper prepared for the American Assembly volume *Women in the American Economy*, August 1975.

35. MOSES, Yolande. Female Status and Male Dominance in Montserrat, West Indies. Ph.D. thesis, University of California, Riverside, 1976.
36. ——. Female Status, the Family and Male Dominance in a West Indian Community. *Signs*, Vol. 3, No. 1, 1977, pp. 142–53.
37. NEWLAND, Kathleen. *The Sisterhood of Man*. New York, Norton & Co., 1979.
38. NIEVES, Isabel. Household Arrangements and Multiple Jobs in San Salvador. *Signs*, Vol. 5, No. 1, 1979, pp. 134–42.
39. OTTERBEIN, K. The Family Organisation of the Andros Islanders: A Case Study of the Mating System and Household Composition of a Community in the Bahama Islands. Ph.D. thesis, University of Pittsburgh, 1963.
40. POWELL, Dorian. Women in the Caribbean Family. Paper presented at ISER Workshop on the Women in Caribbean Project, September 1980. Mimeo.
41. ROBERTS, G. W. A Life Table for a West Indian Slave Population. *Population Studies*, Vol. 5, No. 3, 1952, pp. 238–43.
42. ——. The Working Force of the Commonwealth Caribbean at 1970. Paper prepared for Seminar on Manpower Planning, Caribbean Development Bank, Grenada, April 1974.
43. ROBERTS, G. W.; SINCLAIR, Sonja A. *Women in Jamaica: Patterns of Reproduction*. New York, KTO Press, 1978.
44. SAFA, Helen Icken. The Female-based Household in Public Housing: a Case Study in Puerto Rico. *Human Organisation*, Vol. 24, No. 2, 1965, pp. 135–9.
45. SAWHILL, Isabel. Discrimination and Poverty among Women Who Head Families. In: Martha Blaxall and Barbara Reagan (eds.), *Women and the Workplace*, pp. 201–12. Chicago, University of Chicago Press, 1976.
46. SMITH, M. G. Education and Occupational Choice in Jamaica. *SES*, Vol. 9, No. 3, 1960, pp. 332–54.
47. SMITH, R. T. *The Negro Family in British Guiana: Family Structure and Social Status in the Villages*. London, Routledge and Kegan Paul, 1956.
48. ——. The Nuclear Family in Afro-American Kinship. *Journal of Comparative Family Studies*, Vol. 1, No. 1, 1970, pp. 55–70.
49. STACK, Carol. The Kindred of Viola Jackson: Residence and Family Organisation of an Urban Black American Family. In: N. E. Whitten and J. F. Szwed (eds.), *Afro-American Anthropology: Contemporary Perspectives*, pp. 303–11. New York, The Free Press; London, Collier-Macmillan, 1972.
50. ——. Sex Roles and Survival Strategies in an Urban Black Community. In: M. Z. Rosaldo and Louise Lamphere (eds.), *Woman, Culture and Society*, pp. 113–28. Stanford, Stanford University Press, 1974.
51. STEIN, R. L. The Economic Status of Families Headed by Women. *Monthly Labor Review*, Vol. 93, No. 12, 1970, pp. 3–10.
52. TANNER, Nancy. Matrifocality in Indonesia and Africa and among Black Americans. In: M. Z. Rosaldo and Louise Lamphere (eds.), *Woman, Culture and Society*, pp. 129–56. Stanford, Stanford University Press, 1974.
53. TRINIDAD AND TOBAGO. CENTRAL STATISTICAL OFFICE. *Eastern Caribbean Region Population Census 1960, Vol. I, Part A: Administrative Report*. Port of Spain, 1967.
54. UNITED NATIONS. Sex Based Stereotypes, Sex Biases and National Data Systems. ST/ESA/STAT/99. June 1980. Mimeo.
55. WEEKES, Hildegarde. One-parent Families with Special Reference to Women's Roles Therein. Barbados, National Commission on the Status of Women, *Report*, Vol. II, pp. 674–93. Bridgetown, Ministry of the Attorney General, 1978.
56. WILSON, P. J. Caribbean Crews: Peer Groups and Male Society. *Caribbean Studies*, Vol. 10, No. 4, 1971, pp. 18–24.
57. ——. Household and Family in Providencia. *SES*, Vol. 10, No. 4, 1961, pp. 511–27.

SS.82/XXIX-2/A